CROSSINGS
Long-term Perspectives of the Troubles

CROSSINGS
Long-term Perspectives of the Troubles

compiled and edited by

An Crann The Tree

Published by An Crann The Tree

BELFAST

2001

Published by An Crann *The Tree*
10 Arthur Street
Belfast BT1 4GD

ISBN 1 898 472 64 5

AUTHOR
An Crann the Tree

TITLE
CROSSINGS
Long-Term Perspectives of the Troubles

COVER DESIGN
December Publications

PRINTED
Noel Murphy

Funded by the European Regional Development Fund

An Crann The Tree was founded in 1994 as a cross-community, charitable organisation to create a respectful space for those affected by the Troubles to tell their stories. Various media are used to share the pain of the past 30 years – poetry, drawing, narrative, painting, drama, video and photography. It is An Crann's belief that only by embracing all perspectives of the Troubles that we can, as a society, break through prejudice and suspicion to rediscover our similarities, respect our differences and chart a fresh course for the future together.

If we could read the secret history of our enemies, we should find in each person's life sorrow and suffering enough to disarm all hostility.

HENRY WADSWORTH LONGFELLOW

Acknowledgements

I am grateful to the contributors who shared their stories and their lives with a total stranger. I appreciate their openness and hospitality as well as their patience with the consent process.

Cathie McKimm invited me to undertake this interview project, gave guidance and instilled the confidence to move forward. Thank you to An Crann's Management Committee for support and encouragement.

Thank you to Gráinne Kelly for words of wisdom and advice as well as her assistance with editing and to Natalie Strain for her technical support and encouragement.

Patrick Ramsay was helpful in explaining the printing process.

Thank you to the Community Relations Council and specifically to Mark Adair, the European Programme Director, for funding the project.

Without the financial support of Mennonite Central Committee, I would not be in Northern Ireland, and I am grateful for the opportunity to work in the field of peace and reconciliation. Thanks to Joe Campbell for suggesting that I work at An Crann The Tree.

Photo Credits

Pages 30, 37 & 77	Photography reproduced with the kind permission of the trustees of the museums and galleries of Northern Ireland.
Page 48	Photography supplied by Sister Baptist.
Page 55	Photography supplied by Elsie Kirkpatrick.
Page 68	Photography supplied by Community Visual Images.
Page 84	Photography supplied by Mary Beattie.
Page 99	Photography supplied by Dermot Walsh.
Page 104	Photography supplied by Jim Snoddy.
Cover photography	Community Visual Images and Mary Beattie.

List of Contributors

Tom	*Tom Hannon*
Lily	*Elizabeth McKenna*
Jean J	*Pseudonym used*
Bernadette	*Bernadette Park*
Sister Baptist	*Pseudonym used*
Elsie	*Elsie Kirkpatrick*
Patrick	*Patrick O'Connor*
Jean	*Wishes to use first name only*
Lillian	*Pseudonym used*
Pauline	*Wishes to use first name only*
James	*James Snoddy*

Contents

Introduction

Thirty years of the Troubles in Northern Ireland have left their mark on all people, but those who are now over 50 have borne a disproportion of the suffering. It is their sons, husbands, wives and daughters who have been targets of bombs and bullets. It is they who have been forced from their homes by intimidation, or they have suffered physical injuries themselves. Sometimes they have needed to care for an injured relative or have watched stress take its toll on someone they love. Fear and uncertainty have been daily companions as they have tried to go about their daily business and have kept life as normal as possible for their children.

Twenty-eight percent of the population in Northern Ireland is over 50. Warm memories of friendships across the sectarian divide, formed when neighbourhoods were more diverse, remain. Not only do long-term friendships dilute prejudice and misinformation, the ageing process itself can have a softening effect, as people grow to distinguish what is truly important.

It has been a distinct privilege – indeed like walking on holy ground – to listen to accounts of lives well lived in spite of difficult circumstances. I have been challenged by the openness, the tolerance and the humanity of those who have endured so much pain. It is also clear that others have lived on the margins of the Troubles, affected only minimally in a personal way.

The wisdom and insight brought to any society by its most senior members are valuable resources, often overlooked. Until memory's stories are written or recorded, they are in danger of being lost forever. These interviews occurred in nursing homes, folds and in a few cases in the storyteller's own home or place of employment. Ages of interviewees ranged from 67 to 93, and an attempt was made to record different viewpoints. Each contributor received a copy of his/her life story from which these extracts were taken. It is with gratitude that I share what was entrusted to me with the permission of the narrators or their family members and hope that you will be inspired, as I have been, by the resilience of the human spirit.

SARA WENGERD

Tom

Tom is the Director of the Cornerstone Community on the Springfield Road, Belfast. Although his own daughter was seriously injured in the Troubles, he is committed to cross-community dialogue and relationships.

I was born in 1933 on the 19th of May, and I am now 67 years old. The first important thing that happened to me was that my mother died when I was ten months old. I had a brother and two sisters, and my father was still alive at that time. He suffered like so many people in Northern Ireland in the 30s with some form of bronchial or respiratory problem. And what happened then was I was brought to live with my aunts. My Aunt Lizzie was my father's sister, and Ned was her husband. Their name was Riley. So they took me as a baby.

Now, as well as taking in myself, my Aunt Lizzie was sort of the matriarch of the family in a way. And she had inherited some instructions from her mother to look after her bachelor brother who lived in the house and to look after the rest of the family. My Aunt Cassie, her sister, also lived in the house with her daughter, because my Aunt Cassie was a widow. There was another sister, my Aunt Sarah, so in actual fact in our little terrace house we had six adults and one child. The unfortunate thing for me was the next youngest was about 25 years older than myself, so I was one child in a house full of adults. Quite a bit of my life was spent steering a course between the likes and dislikes of all these adults.

My father died when I was about six and a half years old, just about the outbreak of the war. The times my Aunt Lizzie used to threaten me when I was being bad with being sent home. I remember saying to her, "You won't be able to send me home now." So this business of, "We will send you home," tended to create a sort of feeling of impermanence in the home.

By that time, of course, I had gone to one of the Catholic schools. The school is just in off the Springfield Road, behind Clonard Monastery. St. Gall's it was called. John Baptist de la Salle founded this order of teaching brothers to teach the children of the poor. So I went to that school, and I was reasonably happy there. My people were very strictly Catholic, and I was continually failing to meet certain standards.

Of course what I didn't realise at the time was that my aunt also had her problems. When my father died, you see, the family broke up. My brother went off to England, and my sisters separated. However, the younger of the two came to live with us, and there were other tensions. There were a lot of tensions in the family, because it wasn't as if we were a proper family in the sense of father and mother.

My Aunt Sarah and I were very close, but then my Aunt Sarah was also disapproved of, and we even had politics in our family. You see my Aunt Sarah was a very staunch republican, whereas my Aunt Lizzie, she was a nationalist. The nationalist member of Parliament was a man called Joe Devlin, and my Aunt Lizzie used to talk about having followed him. In those days, of course, we didn't have television, so you had the election meetings in the street, and she used to talk about following Joe Devlin in her bare feet. Now my Aunt Sarah, being a republican… on one occasion DeValera came to contest the election in West Belfast in 1918 for the republicans, and I remember the rows over who should have washed the dishes frequently ended up with a reference to how one voted in 1918.

There were times whenever I found that my Aunt Lizzie was terribly concerned about what the neighbours thought and that sort of thing. So I was raised up in a rather difficult, thorny situation. I fell between two stools. My Aunt Lizzie would have preferred me to play and to chum around with the nice fellas in the street who were altar boys, and they were always held up to me as being perfect. "Look at them, they are like pins and paper," which was a reference to their cleanliness. The other guys - the rougher guys in the street whom I recognised as being much more honest and straightforward - I tended in that direction. I had a reasonably lonely childhood - did an awful lot of reading - spent an awful lot of time in the library.

I was only about 16 at the time [when Tom's sister came to live in the house], and sometimes I look back and think that I was sometimes quite brutal in some of the things I said to her. But we rubbed along together, and in later life she moved to the United States to live until 1992 when she developed cancer. She was a single woman. She lived in Manhattan and wanted to die at home. So we went out to bring her home [my wife and myself], and she died on the airplane at about half an hour to touchdown at Shannon.

After leaving St. Gall's School, I went to a school called Harding Street or St. Joseph's as was its proper name which is nearer North Belfast and was run by the Irish Christian Brothers. For a good part of the time I was very unhappy there, because I was a timid individual. We had a brother there who was the head brother and one of his famous phrases was, "Fetch me a leather." So you would go into the office and bring down the strap, and you would be beaten - on the hands, of course. It was the way things were done. In this day and age, it would be abuse. They would certainly be prosecuted. But in those days, the old saying was, if you went home and said to your mother, "I was beaten today in school," you were probably likely to be beaten again. I can remember on one or two occasions, sitting in the empty classroom weeping because I couldn't work out some problem in maths or physics – not because I was afraid of being punished but because I was convinced that I was too stupid to solve the problem. But I was raised to think in that way.

I left early in 1948. I would have been 15 at the time. After leaving there, under a bit of a cloud admittedly, I got a job in a chemist shop where I was supposed to be serving my time as an apprentice. But really I was the errand boy. And then I left that, and I went into James Mackies and Sons as an apprentice fitter. They made textile machinery. I went in there when I was 16. I walked up what is now called Springvale for the first time on Monday the 17th of October 1949, and I was in Mackies for 46 years until I came to work in Cornerstone. I was an apprentice fitter and I worked in a couple of local mills for Mackies, erecting machinery - as part of a team of course - because I was only 16 or 17 years old. But then in 1952, I moved into the drawing office and became an apprentice draftsman, and I was in the drawing office until I left, doing different jobs. At one time I was in a charge of a little experimental department, and just before I left the company, I was involved with product safety. Ah dear, dear, there was always the threat of redundancy. I mean I know men who worked in the place for maybe over 30 years who were told on a Friday afternoon not to come back on the Monday morning.

And lo and behold in 1995 I was invited to become Director of Cornerstone. I was a member of Cornerstone for 16 years before becoming Director. I joined in the early 80s.

Sally and I started going together when I was 16. You were reasonably sure of your future. In those days a young man would have started his apprenticeship – "serving your time" as it was called – at 16 years old and would have been pretty sure of finishing at around 21. You came "out of your time" at 21, and you were likely to have been going with a girl and saving up to get married. We used to joke that we worked overtime to save up to get married, and then after the wedding, you continued to work overtime to stay married!

So at that time we got married, I was 22. Sally was 23. We were only a couple of kids for God's sake. And we were married on the 9th of July 1955, and I found Sally weeping because she wasn't pregnant. Our first child was born on the 29th of July 1956. So how quickly could you do it? And I still joke her about that. We lived for awhile with my aunt, and when we moved out, we had the child then – Brian - and we moved into our present house. We are still living in the house we moved into when we got married.

We had six children, three boys and three girls, and we had all the vicissitudes of married life - the problems and the overdraft, and the schooling was going on. There were times whenever it was tough enough. Somebody said to me the other day, "I thought you had a good job in Mackies," and I said, "Yes, I had a good job. The salary was the problem!"

Well, we brought up our children. They went to school. They went to secondary school. They all eventually went to university. They all did reasonably well - settled down after the usual sort of teenage problems and that sort of thing. They all have done well.

But the real problem for us was that about the 15th of December 1969 our youngest son whose name was Gavin was diagnosed as having leukaemia. It meant that we spent an awful lot of time in the children's hospital - The Royal Hospital for Sick Children. And of course the Troubles had started, and there were the riots, and the people were being intimidated out of their houses. The real sort of IRA campaign had not started at that time, but still people were being hurt - people were being killed.

So when we were visiting the hospital, we got to realise that there was an awful lot of what I would call "natural hurt," in the world without bringing more into it with bombs and killing and shooting and what not. You would look at this and you would think, "Look at all these little innocents here. Should we not be spending our time... is this not the enemy? Not each other, but this is the enemy."

We found people of different religions and no religion at all in this awful thing where they had to watch their children suffer and die. However, Gavin died in 1974. He had lived for over four years. He had a gentle enough passing, although he had a lot of suffering, a lot of suffering. It also had an effect on the family, because Deirdre was the next oldest, and I had to say to Sally, "You know, we could be neglecting Deirdre." And they didn't understand. I remember Brian, my oldest boy, going down to see him, and he told me, "Dad, I don't want to go back again." I said, "Well that is understandable - okay, leave it like that."

It [a death in the family] is very difficult. I can remember when my father died. I remember writing this story up because my father died - the sort of things we tell children - he was taken by the angels. I remember writing a little story about it saying, "Is the child not entitled to think that angels are very forward beings, and perhaps a little consultation before they went off with one's father might have been considered?" It is a strange way to deal with it. When he [Gavin] died, I remember us coming home that day from the hospital, and the others had to go to schools and get the other children out of school and tell them. So we had Gavin's funeral, and our friends rallied round of course. Mackies gave me an awful lot of time off to deal with this, because we would spend nights in the hospital.

In October 1975 our oldest daughter, Mary, was shot and crippled. There was a lot of tit for tat killings, and you could be in the wrong place at the wrong time. She was 18 years old, and she was coming from the pictures. Actually she was coming after seeing "The Godfather," coming up the Grosvenor Road. The young fella that she was with pushed her to the ground, but she couldn't get up. The bullet had severed the spinal cord. So she ended up in the Royal Victoria Hospital, and she was there for a month, and then they decided that they would send her to Stoke Mandeville in England. They have a very famous spinal unit there. Jimmy Saville, who was at one time a very famous pop star, did a lot of work for them in promoting this. So she met him while she was there.

Of course we were going to experience a great deal of trouble in visiting, both in terms of travel and in terms of finance. So I was working in Mackies West factory at the time, and I got an envelope one day which contained an airline ticket to London and about £20 in spending money. My colleagues had had a whipround, and I went over and saw Mary and came home and wrote a little note of thanks.

Shortly after that I got another envelope with another airline ticket in it and £40 in spending money, because the people in the main factory had heard about this, and they said, "But we weren't included in this." So they had another whipround. As well as looking at the kindness and support of people, I have to recognise that the majority of people working in those factories were Protestants. So we, as a Catholic family, were helped through that trauma by our Protestant friends. So that was another fillip, another supporting stanchion, of my attitude to violence and to sectarianism and the need again to examine what we were doing wrong that led us into this awful, awful business.

So Mary went there in November, and I visited her just before Christmas in December, and at that time she had got her wheelchair. The regime in Stoke Mandeville was very strict. You worked or you left. They did archery to strengthen the muscles. They did a lot of swimming, and she did well. She also was a very headstrong young woman. The chief surgeon walked in one time, and she had a wraparound skirt on and without saying anything, he pulled this wraparound skirt away, and she clouted him. She said, "Hey, I am a human being here. I am not just something," and he learnt a thing or two.

However, I went to visit her. When I got there, she came wheeling up the ward to greet me, and then she said to me, "How did you get from the station?" I said, "I got a taxi." And she said, "Could we get a taxi and go out?" There was a little panic rising - this is a young woman in this wheelchair. What am I going to do? So I said, "Well look, if you talk to the matron and sister of the ward, and if she says okay, we will go." So she did say okay, so we went into Aylesbury, and we went into some of the shops. Unfortunately the restaurant in Woolworths was a sort of split-level, and I stood looking... the restaurant was down two or three steps. If I had a bit more experience, we could have negotiated... but this lady said, "Do you want to come in?" And I said, "Yes, we do." So she brought us down this ramp, through the kitchens and into the restaurant. But when we got to the restaurant, I queued up. We were too late for lunch, and all that was going on was coffee and sticky buns. I came to her, and I said, "Look is this what you want?" She said, "No." I said, "I suppose you would rather have a fish and chips." She said, "I would rather," so we went out again. And we found one of these places, a little restaurant, and we couldn't get in, but the fella came charging down and said, "All right, all right," and he pulled the door the other way. It was a glass door and it was a sort of swivelling door, and in we got. We had our meal together, and then we got back to the hospital again.

Mary came home for good in February 1976. I went to Stoke Mandeville to bring her home, and we were taken to the airport at London Heathrow in an ambulance. So we got to Heathrow, and they took Mary to the medical centre to board the plane. I was left to take care of the luggage, including the wheelchair and all the bits and pieces which Mary had accumulated over her four months at Stoke Mandeville. Fortunately I was accompanied by a little ambulance lady who was pushing the wheelchair. Some of Mary's bits and pieces were in hospital garbage bags on which was printed, "Hospital Refuse For Incineration." The little ambulance lady was looking around her, taking in all the sights and sounds. She hadn't noticed that one of the bags had fallen open and was leaving a trail of shampoos, talcum powders, bras and knickers all over the departure lounge! Well, we got ourselves righted, and off we went. I met Mary inside the plane, and we went home, and it was great to get her home. Within a fortnight, she was back at work.

We got another handrail in, but we didn't adapt the house. We were talking about it, and Sally went, "We have to do this... we have to move to a bungalow," and I was saying, "This lady will have her own life to live. We have to wait on her." You see the experience that I had in Aylesbury - taking her out - was invaluable. I didn't realise it at the time. I can remember on one occasion bringing her, very pointedly, into the conversation, because a neighbour lady was talking to Sally over Mary's head. I could see that an explosion was about to happen. And shortly after she came home, we were in the town with her, and Sally kept asking her, "Where do you want to go now?" She kept repeating this until Mary lost her temper and said rather sharply, "I just want to shop," much to her mother's dismay. It was at that point that I said to Sally, "That's it. You will have to learn to give help when help is asked for." There was really a very steep learning curve there.

Mary had gone to a sort of a part-time job. You see she was a laboratory technician before she was shot. So she got a job in Lady Margaret Hospital in London, and then she moved to another company on a sort of part-time basis. It was an American company, and they asked her then to go and work for them in Switzerland. She was there for seven and a half years and she worked in St. Gallen. She went there without a word of the language. She worked in St. Gallen - then she moved to Berne.

But she came home from Switzerland and decided that she would go back to university and take a degree, and she went to live in Portrush in student accommodation and took her degree in Coleraine in biomedical science. And she was interviewed on the television because of her history, and I remember her saying to the interviewer, "You know I am not disabled. I just can't walk." She went back and did her doctorate. She married again, so she married, took the doctorate, and had her first baby at 41 - a little girl - she was two years old in July.

But that, of course, brought us to another situation of the effects of violence, and I have to say, had the people responsible for her been at the hospital that night, I don't know that I would have had anything to say to them. I am not sure that I would have forgiven them. She herself apparently had forgiven them, because she told me that she had prayed for them that night - the people who were responsible. She was not a religious person in any sort of formal sense.

Just about in the early 80s my oldest son, who had three children at the time, sold his house. He got the dates mixed up, and he came to live with us with his wife and three children. Sally was called rather earlier than she thought she would be to have a hysterectomy. So after the hysterectomy they said, "now you must go home and convalesce." Our little semi-villa was bulging at the seams, so Cornerstone gave us a room, and we came to live in Cornerstone. Now Cornerstone was just going for a few years. I think the first people moved into Cornerstone in 1982. This would have been 1985, I think. So that was our introduction to Cornerstone.

Now we were well aware of it, because it sort of generated out of what was called Christian Life Communities, a Catholic organisation run by a lady called Mary Grant in Northern Ireland - a Catholic sister in fact. Mary was one of the prime movers in establishing the prayer group that later became Cornerstone. But we moved in. We were here for about five weeks - over an Easter period - so people would have gone on holidays.

Sally had made a couple of attempts to go out and had found it difficult. She had tried it too early, but she certainly was recuperating. We got some sort of idea of what the community was doing, and then the community invited us to join. Well, we both did, but Sally later was to be regarded more as a friend of the community than a member. So as I told you, that went on until 1995 whenever the community invited me to become Director when Sam retired. Sam was my predecessor. Sam is a Methodist minister.

That brings us up to 1995, and I have been director ever since. Of course, as I say, because of the pressures in Mackies at the time, it was a Godsend - it really was a Godsend. I felt that. The words of the Psalmists used to form part of my prayer - "What shall I render to the Lord for all that he hath rendered to me?" Now there are pressures in this job. There are pressures, and there are pressures within communities. I am amazed at just how many of us are victims of either childhood or some relationship along the way - whether it is a marriage, a family relationship that impacts on our attitudes. You know one of the things that I have tried to teach myself is to ask myself, "Why am I feeling like this?" I think it is Abraham Lincoln who is accredited with this saying - "I don't like that man. I must get to know him."

In the Divine Office we say a prayer which says, "Free us from the evil that lies hidden in our hearts." And frequently when I am going along very nicely, the evil that lies hidden in my heart comes up and bangs me on the back of the head with a lead pipe! I am still a practising Catholic. You went to confession - you went to communion - the two things were linked. And it was always regarded as wrong if you didn't go to communion the next day. This creates a notion that you must be good before you approach God. What it means is that you then do not go to God and say, "Lord I'm not handling this well - help me."

I remember saying to a priest one time, "Father, what bothers me is that people look at me, and they say I am a good man. Tom is a good man," and I say, "I know that I am not." And he said, "Codswallop. There is a lot in your life that is good, a lot of it," and he said, "If you don't recognise it, how will you thank God for it?"

That's liberating. It also means that you can open the dark side, and when we want to approach God again, we go to confession, and it would be all right. So I think I have got to the stage now where I say, "Right Lord, I am feeling this - I am feeling angry. I am feeling lustful. I am having these sexual fantasies that I don't want." Christoph Arnold in his book, "Dealing With Sinful Thoughts," says, "The pigeons fly overhead. You don't have to invite them to roost in your hair."

Cornerstone started off as a prayer group of Protestants and Catholics from the Shankill and the Falls - brought together by Mary Grant, Rev. Bill Jackson and Rev. Sam Burch - their moving into Clonard and calling themselves the Clonard Group. That continued for seven years with a meeting once a fortnight. But during the seven years, we had the hunger strikes. Now the hunger strikes divided even further an already divided community, and the little Clonard Group also felt the tension because - now this is a generality of course - but Protestants were opposed to the hunger strike. The Protestants in the group might have seen these young men as being exploited by the godfathers of the IRA - that is how it was put. The Catholics, while not agreeing with the method - not agreeing with the actual starving to death - would have seen the end of political recognition as legitimate. So you had the tension, and I am told in some cases, it became quite vociferous. But at the end of each meeting, they would pray together - they would embrace - and they would agree to come back to the next meeting. So it went on for about seven years, and they then thought that they were being called to come more closely together in some sort of lived-in community.

Our first people moved in just before Christmas 1982. There were two Catholic sisters - Mary Grant of course, as the sort of prime mover and rather charismatic figure and Sister Gladys Haywood who was English and a sister of St. Francis. She was a nurse and had done most of her work in Ghana and had retired back to Belfast here. And the other one was Hazel Dickson who was a Methodist teacher. They were later joined by a young lady called Mary Clare Campbell. So they were our first lot, and obviously the community has grown and contracted. We are still here and we hope we are a witness of Christ's reconciling love on this peace line by actually living together.

I suppose it is true to say that what probably was one of our big outreaches was the bereavement visiting that took place when the Troubles were at their height. What started it off was the murder of a young man called Taggart. He lived not too far from here on the Shankill Road. He was a member of the UDR [Ulster Defense Regiment]. But he was shot by the IRA, and Father Gerry rang up Sam and said to him, "I would like to go and visit the family." Sam would admit himself that he wasn't at all keen… a bit apprehensive about this…taking a Catholic priest onto the Shankill Road at a time like that. But Gerry was insistent, so the two of them went. The young widow was just a bit too distraught to appreciate what was happening, but they went to the boy's parents whose house was in the same street.

Now Gerry had brought with him a little carving of the head of the Christ - a sort of crown of thorns that somebody had brought him from Chile. This was a strange thing, because that sort of thing among good Ulster Protestants would be regarded as idolatrous. But Sam went in. They introduced themselves. Sam introduced Gerry. The mother and Gerry embraced, and Gerry offered her the little head of the Christ. And as they embraced, they were weeping. The tears fell on the little woodcut, and it looked as if the Christ was weeping for his people. Now that is the sort of story that enthuses us - that inspires us - and that was the beginning of it.

There have been others. We have tried to react to some of the atrocities. One of the others was whenever Philomena was shot in the chemist shop down the road here. Two fellas came on a motorbicycle, and they went in and just shot her dead. Philomena was well known across the divide, because she delivered oxygen cylinders to people who have had respiratory problems. Why they chose Philomena, nobody knew. We held a little prayer service outside the chemist shop one evening, and people came along. Shelagh and I were doing the prayers through a loud hailer. I think Gerry Adams turned up. David Kerr came up to me while I was there, and he said, "You know, Tom, Cornerstone has shown us again." Because all we did was provide, if you like, a little forum of prayer that people could come to, and they could pray about the situation, and they could also say, "We don't want this." One man climbed over the wall from the Shankill Road to say, "I have come here to let you know that not everybody in my community supports this."

And the other story was the story of John Judge. John was shot after his son's birthday party. He was seeing someone off and leaning over the gate whenever the car came in and shot him dead. And we heard about it, and so we went down. Now in that sort of situation, if it were appropriate, we would pray with the people. But of course, being sensitive to what is going on is the important thing. We were hoping for a prayer meeting in the house. We had

Patricia [John Judge's wife] here just to work out how we would do this. It was a fairly emotionally charged meeting, and people were trying to be sensitive. There was a ring at the door, and I went to the door, and there were two children. They said to me, "Do you have a goldfish bowl?" And I said, "No, I don't have a goldfish bowl. What do you want with a goldfish bowl?" And they looked up at me, and they said, "For a goldfish." Now they had obviously bought this goldfish in the city. After a bit of searching around in the garage, we dug out an old enamel casserole dish or pudding basin. They went away carrying this, happy as Larry. I came away from the door, thinking to myself, "What is the Lord saying to us here?" Here on one side of this house we are discussing with Patricia how to commemorate her husband's brutal death, and at the other side we are giving two kids a goldfish bowl to house a goldfish! It said a whole lot of things about the ethos of this house and the fact that they had the confidence to come along and ask us for a goldfish bowl - and that Patricia could come and discuss with us her husband.

We had a prayer meeting in the Woodvale Park, and there was a shower of rain during it. And after the prayer meeting, there was a great double rainbow. It stretched right across Belfast. So these things enthuse us, and when we are feeling a bit down, we tell our stories again.

One man said to me, "How do you pray together?" And I said to him, "Have you ever heard of the Lord's Prayer?" And I said, "Look doctrine and that - that is not the problem. What is more than likely to happen is somebody is likely to say, 'Who left the kitchen in a state?' or 'Who borrowed the sellotape and didn't bring it back?' " You look at the fruit that people produce, and you say to yourself, "Look at the lives that people lead. This is produced out of their traditions - out of their faith. Who am I to question that?" I can see the fruit is good. I am not trying to say that doctrine is not important. I remember somebody saying, "We do have a creed, but let's look at the creed as praise of God, not just as a whole list of things we believe, like a shopping list - a shopping list of belief." That is not the way human beings operate.

Lily

Ninety-three year old Elizabeth McKenna has spent all of her life in Belfast where, as a child, the family was intimidated out of their home. She is the mother of twelve children and now lives in a nursing home.

I was born in Belfast in a street called [I think I'm right] Bute. B-U-T-E. Bute Street. It's on the Shore Road. I was born in 1907 on the 19th of March which makes me 93. Too bad, isn't it? My father was a bricklayer. He was a builder and worked very hard for his family. And he worked all his life as a bricklayer. My mother didn't work any - she just kept the house. My mother had 11 children, and I had 12. I beat her by one!

Well, I went to school as a four year old, not too far from home. And school then was pretty stiff – wasn't soft at all – it was pretty stiff. So I went from class to class 'til I reached the sixth grade - wasn't too bad, but I didn't go any further. After I finished school I went to work. I went to work at 14½ at the factory – a linen factory not too far from home on the Shore Road. Well, you were called a weaver. You weaved the material. It was like threads until it turned into linen. It went from loom to loom. You done so much, and they done so much and so on. It was hard work and very little pay. I think I had one pound a week. Isn't that awful?

[For play as a child] we just went out in the street. You weren't allowed to cross the road. You weren't allowed to leave the street. My mother was very fussy like that, and you played in the street. You were called in for dinner. Then you went out again to play. Then you played until about five o'clock, and you were brought in and washed, and your hair combed to see if it was clean in case there were other kids had a dirty head.

On one occasion my mother found a vermin – lice – one in my head. She nearly went crazy. She took me to the doctor's, and he took me up to the clinic. He sent me up to the clinic where you're liable to get vermin with kids going around – maybe not clean heads, maybe not a clean house. So you could rub shoulders with somebody with lice on their shoulder or somethin' like that. But I got rid of it anyway. My mother was very fussy, very fussy. It's terrible to see children goin' about like this [scratches head]. Poor kids. It's not their fault. It's not the poor kids' fault.

My childhood memories are pleasant enough. As a child when you're with your mother and father, you think you're on top of the world. When you've a good father and mother, it means a lot. I know poor kids that don't have good fathers and mothers. The father drinks, and he comes in and cuts up rough – abuses the children and stuff like that, you know. I didn't experience any of that. My father come in – he took a drink – and he was a lovely step dancer, lovely step dancer. And he used to say to me, "You like dancin'." He says, "Come on, Lily, get up." And then he would have sung "Lily of Laguna." And the two of us would have step danced. And I thought that was great. He was a good father.

My father and mother were different religions. My mother was Catholic, and my father was Presbyterian. But I couldn't say a bad word about him. He worked all the days of his life, and he worked hard. I didn't experience any conflict between my parents over religion which was a good thing too. No, he didn't go to Mass, but he never stopped us from going. Somebody had to take the reins. We coulda run the streets and had nothing – no thought of God or anything. But my mother took hold and she done it all. He was a good father too – worked very hard, so he did.

When I was a child you eat what was set down to you, and if you didn't eat it, you done without. My mother was strict that way. But you never starved, you know. She was very good that way. She baked. She baked, and she done all kinds of food, you know, made the very best of food. And we eat that. When we didn't eat it, we done without, I can assure ye. See my father always worked and handed in his pay packet. My mother was a good manager. She didn't drink, and she didn't smoke or things like that, so we got on okay.

We had a house. We had the three bedrooms – two large bedrooms and a small one, what we called a "box room." But they were occupied. There was two beds in each room, and the small room held a double bed and a single bed. So we done all right, but here I am - I'm still alive.

When you think of it – some kids run on the streets, and they don't care what happens to their children. But my father did. That's why he was pretty strict. Of course I'd rather have the strictness. There's a lot of kids are ignored by their parents. They can run the streets, go to a pub – sit in the pub, drink. The mothers don't care, like I know that much. So I appreciate what my father was… and my mother too. So it's good to have good parents – fairly strict – but good. You realize it all afterwards. You say, "My mummy's very strict." Then you say, "Well, she was right. In lots of things, she was right."

I met my husband Gerard in a dance hall. That's the usual place. But my father didn't allow us to dance – very strict. You weren't allowed to go to dances, yet the hall that I danced in, HE BUILT IT! And he says, "Whenever I get one of you kids in that dance hall, I'll kill youse." But we went behind his back, but that's all ever we did do behind his back.

[Her husband's family] lived not too far from me, and they came to where I did live. And they had a garage and a lot of cars. I thought he was well off. Well, they was in a way. But... I just took the rough with the smooth.

But I got married in the Catholic Church. Oh, I hadn't a big wedding. My father didn't believe in big weddings. I had just an ordinary dress. And I remember the buttons up the back of it, and the people in the church counted the buttons on my jacket. I could hear them! And one woman says, "Would ya mind gettin' up na?" I says, "What fer?" She says, "You're sittin' on a button." [She was trying to count them.] Ah, ye get many a laugh too.

Yeah. Oh, well... the years go by, and you think back and say, "What did I do this for? Why did I do that?" No, I wouldn't change.

I had lots of friends, lots of friends. I used to sing a lot. I was in New York one time, and my name was called. I don't know how they got it. My name was called from the stage. Well, I happened to be one of the ladies in the stalls. And this lady called me up, and she said, "Would you like to sing?" I says, "I can't sing." "Oh yes, you can sing." I said, "Who told you I could sing?" "Well I was told you could sing," so I had to sing. But for the life of me, I can't remember the two songs that I sung. But I sung them right through. And I got a big clap.

I sang in a church choir. I was an alto singer. I was an alto singer, same as my mother. She was a wonderful singer, so she was. Great. But, oh I never stopped singing. I would sing washing the dishes and stuff like that, you know. I love to hear people sing - I really do.

Well, the first one [of her own children] was born Frank. The next one was Jim. And the next one was Louis. He died of a brain haemorrhage. Then later – a few years later – I had another son died with a brain haemorrhage, exactly the same thing, what you call an aneurysm. Well, it's one of those things that happens. They were in their 20s. Yes, it was sad. Indeed it was sad... but you have to get over these things. It nearly killed me but... you get over it. You don't get over it. You don't ever get over it, I don't think. Yes, well God wanted them, and he took them. That's the way I look at it. God wanted them, and he took them. Sure it is very hard. It took a long time. It took a long time [to come to terms with their deaths]. No, it's no joke, losing a child. No matter how young they are or how old they are or whatever, it's a big loss. Well, when I lost these children, I got over it pretty good, but I always asked God to help me. "Oh, God, please help me get over my loss." So He did.

Well, they [friends and family] come in and took me out, and you know, things like that - and took me to somebody's house and have a yarn, you know talk about different things so... these things crop up. My husband talked very little about it, but he thought too much. He thought a lot, so he did.

I had seven boys and five girls. [The boys are] Frank, Gerald, Patsy, Maurice, Jim, Louis and Alouisus. [The girls are] Maureen, Sheila, Pauline, Margaret and Nuala. Oh, they're wonderful. I have a wonderful family, I must say. They do anything for each other, and I think that's marvellous - good family, well brought up. Not spoiled - I couldn't afford to spoil 'em. But they were all very good. But don't ever tell 'em I said it!

There was no trouble. None - not even the boys. Nobody ever came to the door and said, "Mummy, here's a policeman wants to talk to you about somebody beat somebody, you know." I never had that trouble, thank God.

It was great. Great [to have 12 children in the house]. I could manage them all. I managed every one of them and managed them well – cooked for them, baked for them, washed for them. And I asked nobody to help me, thank God. Isn't that wonderful?

Oh, God save us. Typical day – well one would come in and say, "Mummy, so and so hit me." "Run away now and give me peace. I don't want to fight with the children outside." I wouldn't fight with anybody's child, because mine were as bad as they were. Well, that's the way I looked at it, and so they were – all wee devils, I think, but there you are. Never give up. Got up in the morning, made the breakfast, got the kids washed and dressed for school – the ones that went to school. Well, when I got the kids all out to school, the ones that went to school, I started to wash all the clothes that come off their back. I left nothing dirty, and then I done the baking. I baked every day. Every day I baked bread – soda bread, wheaten bread, and then I baked bread in the oven, oven bread. There's not very many young women bake today. They wouldn't know how to bake. See my mother baked all her life. She baked all the bread that we eat. I followed suit. It's true. But didn't do me any harm. Didn't do me any harm. So... there we are.

Caring for the children took a lot of time. I never got a minute. But I thought it was my duty to do that, and it *was* my duty. I brought those children into the world, and it was my duty to do all these things for them, and I thought nothing of it, nothing of it. So... thank God. God's good. God's good.

I have good faith. I'm a Catholic, and I wouldn't change my faith for nobody. Now I don't object to anybody being of other religion. I respect all religions, every one of them. I respect them all. But there it is - I would change my faith for nobody. I think it's a worthwhile thing. It really is. It's worthwhile, but God's good. I always say that. I just say things my mother used to say. "God's good," and then she'd say, "The devil's not bad, you know!" Ahh, dear, dear.

The Troubles were bad. If you were a Catholic, some Protestants hated you - vice versa. But I hated nobody, nobody. God bless us, I never hated anybody - never, never hated anybody. That's why God's good to me, and no matter who my kids brought in, I never asked them what religion they were, what school they went to. They were their friends, and that was it, and I think that's the way life should be – just be good to them, you know.

We lost our home. We were put out. We were either put out or burned out. "If you don't get out, we'll burn you out." I've seen people getting burned out. I seen one person getting burned out, and they threw her very cat on top of the fire. God, it was terrible. How people can hate - it's not in me. I can't help thinkin' about it – how they hate one another, because they're one religion or the other religion. Sure we're all God's children, so we are. We're all God's children, one way or the other. It's a shame.

Well, three men came to the door one Sunday afternoon. My mother was standing at the door. Now she went to the door, and I stood behind the glass door to see who was at the door, because they were always wondering who was comin' or what trouble they were gonna bring. So I heard them sayin', "You have ta get out of this house. We'll give ya 'til Tuesday ta get out, and if ya don't get out by Tuesday, we'll burn ya out." That was it... so we got out.

We went to a wee house in Greencastle, a miserable lookin' wee hole. But it was a cover. It was a shade, you know. What age was I? I can't remember? I wasn't very old. I was somethin' like 12 or 13, somethin' like that. Well, I wasn't too bad. I was too young to understand the real thing, you know. But there it is... that's where we ended up – in Greencastle - in a wee house. But thank God, we escaped. We escaped it. We stayed in Greencastle a long time. We got a decent house then, you know.

The Troubles weren't easy. That was all through religion, religion – Catholic and Protestant. Not the good people, now, not the decent people. But it's hard to believe that anybody could hate ya, because you're a Catholic or anybody could hate ya, because you're a Protestant. It's not in me to be like that. I can't be like that.

[The boys were never involved in paramilitary activities.] My sons were very, very broad-minded, thank God. Thank God. They were all good like that. Well, I used to say, "You're a Catholic. Ya have to love your neighbor, do good to them..." My mother taught me this. "Do good to them that hate you. Bless them that curse you. And pray for the people who persecute you." And that always stuck in my mind, and I worked on that. I don't think it was a bad thing to do. No... 'cause my mother was very broad-minded.

My father was a Protestant – Presbyterian. One of the best, he was indeed – a good man, good father. Worked all his life for the children... brought in his wage packet, and that was it. He was a lovely singer, and he was a lovely step dancer. That's the way he entertained us. He never come in fightin', oh no. It's good ta have thoughts like that.

[Gerald died 13 or 14 years ago.] It's terrible. It's no easy joke. It's not easy bringing up children on your own. But thank God, I always say, "God's good, and so He is." He's about 14 years dead. I can't remember what age he would be. [The children were] fairly grown up. Well, I can't remember what killed him, what he died with, but it was a big loss, terrible big loss. I used to waken up in the middle of the night talkin' to him. It was terrible. I missed everything – comin' in every night from work. He'd a got washed and shaved. My husband never sat down to a meal without bein' washed and cleaned. And he wouldn't have touched food with his dirty hands. Ach, people talked nice about him, you know. He was good lookin'. I think I was 19^{1}/$_{2}$ when I got married. Gerald went off to the army soon after we were married. The children were all born afterwards. He was gone something like five years while I stayed at home. We were the sufferer.

I must say, I have a marvelous family – wonderful family, and I couldn't say anything different. Well, I was good to me mother. We were all good with each other. And I suppose that was a sample. Oh, I always believed in treating people decent, whether they deserved it or not. It taught them a lesson to be good to other people. That's what I think. That's the God's truth. I couldn't say a bad thing about anybody, whether they deserve it or not. And it's not fair - it's not right. And it sets a bad example. Yes, yes indeed, I can look back on my life with satisfaction.

Jean J.

Jean came to Northern Ireland from Co. Monaghan after the death of her grandmother. She lived in east Belfast during the height of the Troubles, rearing two daughters. She remembers the UWC Strike and the looting of a chapel nearby. Jean is in her 80's.

I was born in Co. Monaghan of a poor working family. I was the oldest. My mother had twins in a short space of two years and then two others. My granny reared me. We lived close beside each other, but my granny really was my mother, because my mother had a handful - five girls like. We lived on a small farm - a couple of cows, some hens, couple of sheep - everything in small quantities.

I have very happy memories. My grandmother was wonderful. She was a caretaker of a Presbyterian church which still stands to this day. We hadn't much, but we had a happy childhood.

We went to a mixed school. Our neighbours were Catholics, and we went arm-in-arm, hand-in-hand to school and came home from school the same. Everybody knew everybody. There was no such thing as, "You are me, and I am you." There were big families. Further up the road there was a 15 family and just at the bottom of the road there was a 14. You knew you were a Protestant or a Catholic. You never said, "You are this one, or you are that." We never had that. It is a different atmosphere from here altogether. You just automatically went to your place of worship – the way you were reared. It wasn't a dividing. We all knew and respected your religion. When they were working on the farms - say you were cutting hay today - somebody would have gone to help you, and then tomorrow they would have come back. There was no payment or anything. It was automatically that one neighbour helped the other.

My mother died when she was 32, so we were all split. The twins went to a home in Dublin. The other granny reared the two young 'uns. The baby was 18 months, and my mother's sister took me across the border to Fermanagh. That's why I went up to the North.

My father had died earlier. I actually can hardly remember my father. My grandmother was father and mother and everything to me. After my grandmother died, an aunty took me. She was a third mother, if you could call it that really. She had two of her own family, but she treated me well. Then I

35

came to Belfast when I was able to work. There was no such thing as going on to college or anything. You just didn't do it. You had to go to work. You hadn't the same chance. I went to service in a big house 'til I met my husband.

I met my husband at the pictures, believe it or not. There was no such thing as you went for supper or anything else. The boys had no more money than we had, and then we married. I had my one girl, and then I had the second girl - two girls, two lovely girls, thank God, and two lovely son-in-laws - four grandsons. I am a great grandmother three times. I have four grandsons, and I must say I idolize them. They will come in just and throw the arms round me. I am blessed in that way like, I must admit. Any hardships I had has been compensated over the years, because I have a devoted family in every way.

He [Jean's husband] was a deliveryman with a lorry, a big lorry - the Co-Operative. He died of a heart attack. That was 1944, 'round about 42 [years of age]. The girls were ten and twelve. It was hard for Alice especially - she was devoted to her daddy. She took it very bad, but she got over it, like.

But I had to go to work then - there was no other option. I had known this shop, and I had gone down, and Mr. Kelly was looking for somebody for Christmas. They let me work in with the children at school - flexible hours - and I had two of them educated, well educated. They done their secretarial, the both of them. Alice got married - met a lovely fella from the country. Iris has been a Christian all her life. And her and this boy went to school together, and neither him nor her had any romances, and Iris came in, and she says, "Mummy, I think we will get engaged." Then I was on my own. They were my life for years, and I must admit we had happy days.

Well, it [working] was hard - we had long hours. It was no such thing as nine to five. At a holiday time, you could have worked until 11 or 12. You had no privileges [retirement benefits or pension plans] like what they have nowadays. Of course there was nothing like that anywhere. There wasn't anything like the widow's benefit. When I was in the shop, the girls - Alice especially - used to help Mr. Kelly to do the invoices and different wee bits and pieces. And they were allowed to come down to me in the shop which meant an awful lot.

Well, the Troubles has been bad. We were put out of work three or four times - closed the shops - everybody out [during the UWC strike]. And actually I was nearly getting caught up in the trouble that day. They hijacked all the vans and put them across the roads where our shop was, and we were told to get out. Well, there was three of us had to walk up the road, and there was another barricade, but we weren't going through that. I was always a wee bit hot-

headed. I says, "What do you mean, I'm not going through? I'm going home."
I had two daughters. I was going home. I says, "I am going home," and this
wee skitter - excuse the expression - says to me, "You can't go through." "Well,"
I said, "who is your boss?" And this crowd of big toughs were standing over in
a bakery shop. He says, "He's there," and I says, "You tell him I want to see
him." The wee woman that I worked with, she said, "Come on Jean, we'll go
back down to Kellys - come on." I says, "No, no I am going home in spite of
them." Well this big fella came out, and right enough, I was terrified, you know
- I was terrified. He says, "What do you think is wrong with you?" I says, "I
want home - that is all I want. I have been put out of work. I want home."
"You can't go through." "Oh," I says, "Can I not? Well I am going through,
and if you want to stop me, you do it." I put my foot over the thing, and he
said, "Oh go ahead, go ahead." Anyway I got in home, and I just collapsed with
shock. I was a brave girl like, when I was down.

But there was one terrible event around Easter time. There is a lovely chapel
up there [points to the road]. Well, the chapel hadn't been long opened - a
beautiful place, and they raided it. I was in bed with a migraine that day. I
never had the like of it, and I could hear this racket, and I am sorry to say it,
they took the very statues and threw them onto that road which was terrible.
Actually the Protestant people at that time collected for the chapel, and some of
them went and scrubbed, including myself, because we were ashamed actually.
I had wonderful friends and neighbours - still have some of the friends from
Thyme Road which were put out unfortunately, like. They had to move - they
had to move down to the Strand. But that chapel incident - I think it was
broadcast over the world. It had every right to be broadcast, because it was
terrible. I mean a place of worship is a place of worship. It doesn't matter what
you are or who you are, I don't think it should be interfered with.

Well then, the shops gradually started to open. You see, the shops and
everything were scared to open. And then, even when the strike was over, they
were ransacking everywhere. Oh, the Troubles were bad - everybody was
stressed out. You never knew one morning till the next. And then when the
army moved in, it put an awful strain on you. Now east Belfast gets a wild name
- call it what you like - but there never was any of that, and that come when the
army moved in. You felt terrible. They moved into our area. They were there
for your protection, yes, but you really felt uncomfortable. Oh aye, it was bad.
But then it was both sides was bad - it wasn't one or the other. Stuff was scarce.
You would hardly have got a loaf or milk or anything. There was no deliveries
or anything. You had to sort of nearly beg for to get a loaf.

[The neighbours helped one another during this time.] There was one fella worked in McConnell's, a big fruit place and John, if he had had anything, would come over and slip me... he had to literally slip like, you know. The atmosphere was bad. You felt tense. You felt horrible about it.

[The young kids] were the worst. You would have saw six and eight year olds stoning. One minute they would have been stoning the army. Then the next thing it would have been the police. Some of them [army and police] came in to help you, and they were actually stoning the fire brigades and all that sort of thing, which was uncalled for. It didn't really make any sense. And the kids started trouble. That's why we could never understand why the kids were allowed out. We could never understand. If my children had've been younger, they wouldn't have been allowed out. It was as easy as that. But then it is different generations you see.

[Jean was afraid for her children's safety.] They were all on the road as the saying is. Like Jack, Alice's husband, he is a petrol driver. And Alistair, Iris's husband, he is a rep. He does north and south for a firm. So you had the strain all the time... wondering. When I had got the phone, always they phoned and used to say, "I am home safe and sound." You just used to say, "Thank God." They were very fortunate. Jack drove through all the Troubles. He lost the tanker a couple of times, but he never was touched. When you think about the destruction, the poverty it put people into...

We stayed out [of Belfast city centre]. You didn't go into the town centre, unless you really had to, because there was searches on everywhere - before you went into the shops and when you came out. It was horrible when you think of it now, right enough.

You just hoped and prayed every day that everything would be all right. It is funny how you can adjust to things. Many's a time you wonder how you really got through it. And yet our church went on and all my family is very open-minded. Their motto is, and I think it is the way they are reared, "Live and let live." She [Iris] would say, "We are all on this earth together - we all live together. You will be judged according to how you have lived." I do believe everybody is entitled to their own religious outlook, and I do believe if you are reared, you should live what you are reared. If you hadn't faith, you would be lost. Now I am not professing that I am a good Christian. I don't mean that, because I think you have to be a good Christian to profess one. But I do believe in God, and I do believe that He looks after you, no matter where you are.

Sometimes you hadn't clothes to go to church - proper clothes. But my children always went to church dressed, and that wee Catholic neighbour of mine loved to see them going out. I says to her one morning, "Hey, does youse not go to Sunday school?" She says, "Jean they don't have to go to Sunday school. I get mine up at half seven and they go to Mass." We always would… even if I see her yet… we have a debate. But she informed me that she could get hers at half seven where I could get mine out for eleven o'clock. If you hadn't trust, or if you hadn't faith, where would you be? And I do think that is what's wrong with people - our churches are down very badly, unfortunately.

[Jean has visited the Presbyterian church in Co. Monaghan where she attended as a child.] The church is still there, and two years ago just they got heating in. There was a big stove in the middle of it that my grandmother used to fill with timber. I have photographs taken at that church. There was dry rot in the pulpit one time, and they collected to get it all repaired. And the first name on that list was £100 from McCarneys, the Catholic family beside us. Now that is honest truth.

[Jean comments on growing older.] Well, there is no hardships like, I can put it that way. But nobody likes to get old - believe you me, you don't. [Jean suffers from angina.] There is a valve somewhere not functioning properly. I am just happy and contented that pensioners are being looked after - very comfortable - most of them. I have a family second to none. Now they are not always lovey-dovey Nanny like, you know. They are there at any time, day or night - son-in-laws and all. I have no regrets, because I have had a good, full life.

Bernadette

Bridie Park was injured by a series of bombs, which were detonated by the IRA in the afternoon of the 21st of July 1972. Twenty devices exploded in a short period of time around Belfast, causing nine fatalities and injuring 130 others. Numerous women and some children were among the casualties. The day is remembered as "Bloody Friday." At nearly 80 years of age, Bridie lives in a fold in Greenisland.

I was involved in a bomb in 1972 - in July 1972 in the afternoon near Cavehill Road where I lived - not far from where I lived. I just went out one day on a short trip, just shopping. And I'd go by bus, so I went down to the bus stop and was just standing a few minutes at the bus stop when the bomb went off.

And I don't remember - I didn't see anything or know anything until I was just lying on my back. And a man came over to me who was driving past in the lorry, and he moved me. I think he probably moved me off the road or not so far out on the road, and then I blacked out again. And a doctor apparently came along and gave me an injection, and I was just so stunned. I didn't feel anything or anything like that.

But I remember being put into the ambulance, and then I blacked out again. And then I came to in the ambulance, and I remember going around a corner with just the sirens going really hard. I knew I was going into the hospital, but the nurses or the doctors apparently were asking my name, asking me what my name was. But I didn't answer them, because I didn't hear them. So it must be some time after that that I knew I was in the hospital then. I was in intensive care.

When I was on the ground, I looked down and I could see one leg, and the blood was just gushing out of it. And it wasn't until much later that I realised that both my legs had a compound fracture in each of them, and I had to go for x-rays first. [My chance of survival] was 50/50, I think. My husband was told, you know, it was 50/50.

I fell on my head, and I have a fair bump. You can see the mark on my head. But, no, just my legs were injured, and I went to the theatre to get the two of them off. They thought they would have to take the two of them off; but luckily they saved the one, and they took the other one off. Yes, he was going to take two of them off, and he took one leg off, but the other one he was able to put into traction to save it, so it saved my life really.

Twenty bombs went off in 20 minutes. They put a lot of the bombs on at that time. They've never been found. It was the IRA. I hadn't come back home... I hadn't come home, and they [my family] just wondered where I was. They knew, of course, that the bombs were going off - the bombs were very bad. When I was taken to the hospital, they didn't know where I was, and apparently although I heard them [medical personnel], my voice didn't come out. My voice was too weak, so they didn't hear what I was saying. My eldest daughter came out with one of the nuns from her convent and went round to hospitals, and that's how they knew I was there. Sometime, but not in the same spot, another bomb went at the same time and killed a child called Parker. And they thought with my name being Park, they thought we were connected. But then they cleared that up, although I did know the lad who was killed.

Well, I have six children. Most of them were home for their holidays. The youngest child was ten, and she and I went down - I usually took her with me - but she didn't come. I have an older son, just older than her, and he said, "We're going to buy goldfish," and they went off to get goldfish, and I would see them later on, but I never met up with them.

[After the incident] my daughter was married in England, and she got a house for me, around the corner from where she was living, so Sheila and I...that was the youngest girl... and I went over. I wasn't able to look after them [the children], you know. And then my two sons at the university came over on their holidays. Eventually they moved to England and got married. I stayed there four years and then came back. I just decided that... in the meantime my husband died... I would rather be living here really rather than over there.

The bomb changed my life completely, because having one leg off and the other one in traction - the traction doesn't come off for three months - so I had to stay in the hospital seven months. I had to go and learn to walk again and manage. I was 50 - 50 when it happened. I still can't go out on my own. I wouldn't go anywhere. I've never been able to go out on my own after it happened. I have to go with some of the family, and it's complete - from being independent and looking after a family and seeing to their needs and what they were going to do. I did quite a bit [of housework] for a long time - I did really. I surprised myself how much I was able to do - the wash - of course the washing machine would do the washing, and I even hung the things out on the line. Oh, I was able to go around the house and everything, but going out - I couldn't go any distance or anything - never could. See I have to use two sticks even to walk, and I even broke my leg before I came down here. Before I came down here, I was in a nursing home when they came down and told me I would have to leave.

I never thought of myself moving to a retirement home. I had bought a bungalow for myself, and I had paid half of it, and my daughter was paying the other half - paying it off. But all the family decided that Sheila should have the house and that I should go into a sheltered dwelling - that's what it's called, a sheltered dwelling - so, very comfortable and all but very lonely, just on my own. I cook the food and sit down and eat on my own. You're stuck the same, cooking for yourself and eating. It's not the same, not at all. And I could go out to the garden, and here there's no garden - there's nowhere to go out and walk about in the garden. I mean, when you can't go out, and you can't drive, and I have no near friends that would take me out or anything like that either.

I watch the television, and I read. I just read novels of any kind, you know. Sometimes I have a break between them, but yeah, I read a lot of American books, you know - American authors. I just buy books or have them given to me, but I just don't go to a library. I did a lot of embroidery, a lot of pictures, but my hands would kill me, because I have arthritis as well. I had arthritis before this happened to me. I had it ever since I was 40. And it really destroyed my hands - I can't do embroidery work with my hands.

I've known other people who were affected by the Troubles, but I wasn't friends with them or anything. No, for all the people who were in the Troubles and that, it's surprising, you'd really think you would know more people that something has happened to, but I don't really know any.

I'm a person for keeping it [anger] in me, keeping it in. I have nobody to let it out to anyway. Of course it [the bomb] wasn't set off for me. I just happened to be in the wrong place at the wrong time, you know. I just happened to be there. I didn't take it personally, that part of it.

My injuries came very early in the Troubles. I think it really started in about 1969, and this was 1972. It was unusual to have so many bombs go off at one time. I think it was the people in the street got what happened. Everyone was moving around, you know, and you never knew where... no, it had never been before. I think some people are just unfortunate that these things happen, and others come through all right, you know.

I think it [the Peace Process] will come all right. Yes, I think it will. Ach, it's bound to... Troubles aren't right, one person coming in and hurting another. I think it's a dreadful thing.

Sister Baptist

Sister Baptist lived on the Falls Road in the 1970s and 1980s. Her eyewitness accounts of flying bullets and bomb blasts tell of the personal danger the Dominican Sisters faced. Later she went to teach in Africa from 1988 to 1996.

I was born in Warrenpoint, County Down and lived there until I was 19 years of age. And then I entered with the Dominican Sisterhood, quite near Naas in County Kildare. I spent three years there, and during that time I was received and professed. After one year of profession, we were sent out to community. I was sent up to Portstewart for three years. We are an educational congregation. Our sisters are teaching in the university - and colleges and secondary schools and primary schools and créches and also in SPREAD which is the new religious education movement for the mentally handicapped.

[Sister Baptist made a request to get training in science.] You had to have a companion to walk up to the university. But I couldn't get anybody interested in science at the time. So I was sent then to our home economics college in Sion Hill, and I spent three years there. And after that, I came up to Aquinas Hall [in Belfast] which was a student hostel, and I spent nine years there as matron and burser and trainer factotum. I was sent from there to Dublin, and I spent eight years in Dublin where I began teaching. But while I was there, I decided that I'd like to take a degree, and I started the Open University while I was teaching. So I was in service, a student, and having done that, I was suddenly sent to the Falls Road in Belfast, though I hadn't been on the Falls Road before.

That was in 1970, and the Troubles had started in 1969. Well, things were very turbulent at that time actually, because the memory of the burning out of the Bombay Street was very, very vivid to the people. A group of loyalists came into the street and ordered the people out and set their little homes ablaze, and they had nowhere to go. And they got very little time to take anything with them. It seemed so sudden and so unnecessary at the time.

But that I would say was the beginning of the Troubles. There had been a few other things - a murder of a Catholic man and his girlfriend. I'm not too sure whether she was murdered, but certainly the man was murdered in front of her, as far as I know. There didn't seem to be any reason for that to take place. That was before Bombay, but it certainly caused a lot of hurt and made people realise that the old hostilities were still there.

There were a few of the old IRA still alive, and they began to feel the Catholics on the Falls Road had nothing to defend themselves against these bully boys. And they [the IRA] started recruiting. My understanding of it was that the people weren't interested in the IRA, and they didn't want that kind of thing. The IRA then went into one house and asked them to store ammunition in one of the bedrooms. And they did that in a few houses, and then seemingly they actually leaked the news to the police. How true that is, I don't know, but that's the impression I got that this was happening. And then one evening the army came in to several of these houses and found the ammunition. And then they started raiding all the little houses, breaking down doors, pulling up the floors, pulling out ceilings and leaving the place in an absolute mess and walking out. They found very little, but they [the IRA] wanted the people to turn against the soldiers and the police.

And you have one thing happening after the other. And of course then the loyalists started forming themselves into groups, and the Troubles were on us right up to about 1976. From 1970 to 1976 was a very, very troublesome time – a very frightening time to be in Belfast.

I remember once about 1972 I decided I'd like to get driving lessons, so that I could go down to see my father who wasn't so well. And with my instructor we went out one day, and as we went down the road, we were stopped, because there was a burning bus across the road. So the driver said to me, "Well, we'll turn and go up the road." So we didn't get very far past the convent when we were flagged down and told that there was a gun battle – bullets were flying all over the place – and that we'd be wiser to go home. And up the road there was obviously an army barracks, and that's what was causing the problem there. The IRA were shooting anyone who would approach this place.

I certainly know there was another incident that caused people great strife and trouble and helped them to turn against the government and turn against the soldiers. And that was Internment. [Internment commenced in the early morning hours of the 9th of August 1971.] The Northern Ireland government was still in charge. We did have a parliament here, and Brian Faulkner was the prime minister at the time. And he ordered then that the suspect IRA were to be interned, and of course that caused an awful lot of trouble and hardship on the people, because the breadwinners in those little houses were removed. And also an awful lot of innocent people were taken up that had absolutely nothing to do with the IRA or anything else. But after that, there was very definitely a great upsurge of interest in the IRA. It was the only thing that was going to help them. They felt that everybody was against them. Therefore, they had to have something. They [the government] were actually helping the IRA to recruit for themselves, but they didn't see it that way. And they were very wrong in what they did in taking away so many people.

No trial - they were just thrown into prison, and people found it very difficult to visit their relatives as well. So I think that was about the time that the Maze was built, the huge prison that the government is now emptying. The turmoil was very great at this time, even though the people seemed to take it in their stride. I remember on a few occasions, I went down to see my parents in Warrenpoint. Once I left Newry and got into the valley leading toward Warrenpoint, I felt like a balm was coming over my spirit, and it was then I realised, that I was traumatised by what was going on in the Belfast situation. Belfast was a ghetto of mostly Catholics – very poor and unemployed. And they seemed to be the ones that the government had no compassion or consideration for. It was really pretty dreadful, and of course then the streets were full of armoured cars and soldiers.

I'm not quite sure when the IRA bombs started. But I do remember being out in the grounds when the sirens would go, and these were sirens of the ambulances. The Royal Hospital was opposite. You'd hear one ambulance passing and then you'd hear about ten after each other, and then you would know that something dreadful had happened, possibly in the centre of the town. Then we would go to the radio to hear where the bomb had gone off and what had happened. But we certainly knew about it from our experience. It was a hard life in a sense, when I look back on it, especially when you compare the freedom that we have now to then.

Two other incidents that took place... Broadway was a short road that led down to the M1... the roundabout there was constructed about that time. On the opposite side of the roundabout, there was what we call "The Village" at the beginning of Donegall Road. And it was known to be a place where there were a lot of Unionists. But there were often snipers who would shoot up that straight little road, and at the top of the road, the college was part of our complex. Some of our sisters actually slept there at nighttime. And I remember one of them got a bullet in the wall behind her bed. That was one incident.

Another incident was that a car bomb was placed outside our gates, and it went off. And all the windows were shattered in the convent and in the school on the side facing the road, but fortunately none of the sisters got even a scrape at all. We considered that Heaven looked after us and protected us. But it was a trying time. You were slightly frightened about going out. At that time we always wore our habit and our veil, and you avoided going down anywhere that

Sister Baptist feeds lion cubs in Africa.

was near a district that we would consider to be a Protestant district.

Two other incidents that I can remember from that time - our school was actually quite a well-known school with a very good reputation. And we had quite a number of children coming over from Malone Road. Now they would be dropped at the gate, and their parents would move off then to other things. But one morning a magistrate left off his two children at the gate. And as he was about to move off, a motorcyclist came up and shot him. He was rushed into the hospital, but he died that afternoon. Now that was an IRA murder, because he was a magistrate - he was a judge.

We had another incident of a doctor – very good specialist who treated all patients the same way - who would drop his daughter at our gate, and he would move off and pass across town onto St. Malachy's where he would drop off his son. He had two sons, and he had a friend with him this particular day. And as he was passing over Shankill Road, a shot was fired. The boy was killed, and the father got injured, but not fatally. Obviously he passed by that way every morning, and he must have been known by the ones who shot him. He certainly had nothing to do with the terrorist gangs.

The children were very upset about both incidents. There were hysterics. The headmistress looked after that [comforting the children who saw their father's shooting]. As soon as she got there, she took them into her office, and I think the mother came over and an uncle as well. And they went to see the father then. He wasn't dead at the time, and there was this great hope that he would survive, but he didn't.

One other incident - I was teaching in the back of the school, and the back looked onto an alley. And there was one empty house, and that looked out over the military barracks on the other side. Then one morning one sister was out walking – she was probably saying her prayers, walking in the garden – and a car came in at quite a speed and stopped, and two or three men got out with guns in their hands. And the next thing - they ran over to the wall of the alley, jumped the wall and went into the empty house. And before we knew what was happening, shots rang out. And of course, it was very close to where we were. Well, the children went into hysterics. Some of them had actually witnessed a killing further up the road, and this brought the whole thing back. They knew what the consequences were. And it was very traumatic. I'll never forget it.

Oh, here's one other incident that had a funny side to it. Sister Consuella made an arrangement with the army who were in the barracks, not so very far, that if they ever wanted to come and search the place, we were always willing to give them the keys, and they could come in. We did ask though that they wouldn't come near our grounds while the children were at school or after hours' games. The reason was we didn't want snipers trying to get them [the army]. They could easily have got the children. And I must admit the army was exceedingly good about keeping the regulations that we had made.

But one night about 11 o'clock, we got a phone call from neighbours down the road to tell us that the army was breaking down our gates at St. Rose's. Now St. Rose's was an intermediate school. It was a separate building, and it had its own gate. They were knocking down the gate, so Sister Consuella rang the military and told them, did she not explain that she was always willing to give the keys so that our doors wouldn't be destroyed? So she got an apology, and almost immediately, the army came 'round to collect the keys. They had only got in through the gate, but they hadn't actually got into the school. So they said that they got a "tip off," and they would like to verify if it was true. So she thought it would be a good thing to tell the Archdeacon that this was happening. He said he'd be over, and he would accompany Sister Consuella down to the school, and the two of them would remain there for as long as the army was there so that the army wouldn't plant something and then blame us for it. So they went down, and they stayed there until 2.00 a.m. At 2.00 the major came down to say that they had found something, and they would like for them to come along to see it. And it turned out that it was a *huge* amount of ammunition. It was more bullets than anything else. I think there were two rifles, and the rest was ammunition. But it had been stored in the rafters above the cookery kitchen. Now to get to the rafters, they had to use two ladders, one ladder leaning against a tall press and then another ladder from the press to the ceiling. And how they got in is just still a mystery. But it certainly was a big surprise to two people who went down to prevent a planting, and there they found an ammunition dump! But it was really something that we laughed about for a long time. But the nice thing about it was that the commander understood the embarrassment that had taken place. The next morning he came around with a bunch of flowers.

A few times they found weapons about 3.00 a.m. Then they came to the front door and knocked us up to tell us, so that we would hear it before we'd read it in the morning news or we'd hear it on the radio. Then after awhile, they found that they were disturbing us, so they would do it at 6.00 a.m., just before they released the news.

I was horrified at some of the things that were going on – the killings and what not. I had a religious class, and I would speak out quite openly that this was murder and destruction of property and very much against the Christian values. I got a warning. It wasn't given to me. It was given to the headmistress, and she told me, "You've got to be a bit more careful." So I didn't speak out unless I was asked – some incident came up, and they would ask about it.

We certainly tried to make our place an oasis of peace for the children, and people who came in to the grounds would remark on the peace that we had. One incident... it was in the middle of the summertime, and I was in charge of the cleaners. Everything was out of the classrooms - desks were piled up on top of each other - and this teacher came in, and didn't she bring a friend. And I was so horrified. I couldn't believe it. It was most untidy looking. But the lady said to me, "What peace in this place!"

[The Falls Road was a difficult place to live.] It was particularly from 1972 to 1976. It really was a nightmare. You'd never expect it, but you'd be in bed at nighttime, and bullets would seem to be coming off the walls. It certainly did feel as if there were bullets sort of knocked off the wall. And fairly often during the night that would happen. [Sleep was interrupted.] But not only that, it was the fear - there was a certain amount of fear that we wouldn't know what was going to happen or whether you were going to be injured yourself.

[The peace wall] was necessary at the time, because of the snipers. They'd slip across so easily. Also those little homes went up in flames so easily. I wouldn't say it [violence] decreased immediately. It should have been taken down much earlier and some effort made to bring the people of both sides of the street together. The peace wall went up when a young lad was killed in his bed. It was down in the towers on the Falls Road. I don't know exactly how far up he was, but I do know that they actually shot him through the building. The people were so frightened that they demanded something should be done, and that was why the peace wall went up. You could walk through it, but no car could go through. And of course people would recognise people coming through. They knew immediately when the other person came from the other tradition. Unemployment was very high in the Catholic area, so the men had nothing else to do - only stand around and sort of learn who they were. You couldn't invite a Protestant friend up the Falls Road. She would be too frightened. I think if they realised where she was going, that would be all right. But if they thought that she was there for spying... they tried to find out who the spies were.

One very awful incident took place, not far from our house, when a young soldier was shot. As he lay dying, the women came out and danced around him. That shocked a lot of us. It just shows you how things descend, and I remember someone saying, "Oh, let the devil out, and he'll catch a lot." And we felt the

Troubles brought evil in the sense that evil sort of got into the area, and nobody seemed to notice that it was evil. It became acceptable. That was the hard thing about it.

I became Vice Principal, and I had an office, and one day one of the seniors who came from a little bit further up the road came into my office, and some dreadful thing had happened. The IRA had killed somebody or had done something, and I was horrified, and I let her see I was horrified. And I didn't get the response from her that I had expected. So I said to her, "What's wrong? Would you not think that that's terrible?" And she turned around to me, and she said, "You know, Sister, if I went home and told them all that you tell us, they wouldn't believe me." And I said to myself, "Where is all our teaching going?" Evil became acceptable after awhile.

But thank God, I think things have changed. On the other hand, there are people who have given up the practice of religion. I wouldn't say they've given up the religion. People talk about the fact that churches are not as full as they used to be. It would have started with the Troubles. I feel that a callousness came in, and some of the people felt that the church didn't do enough for them. I don't know what they expected the church to do.

Elsie

Elsie grew up in the Shankill, losing her mother during a night of violence and being intimidated out of her home on the peace line. Nevertheless, she has always maintained friendships across the religious divide. Elsie is a member of the Springfield Road Methodist Church.

I was born on a street not far off the Shankill Road. I have three sisters and one brother, my mother and father. We were pretty poor, because my father could not get work. We actually lived in my grandfather's house which had two bedrooms and an outside toilet. We had a very, very good mother. She had a hard life bringing up a family with so little money. My mother went out and got work cleaning out shops so that we would have shoes on our feet. Then as we got a bit older, my father got a job, and we realised then that we could afford a better house which had two bedrooms and a large attic which held the four girls. My brother got the one bedroom and my mother and father in the other room.

We were brought up so well. When we went to live in Silvio Street, there were old people lived beside us who couldn't have gone out for messages. And they might have sent word over to ask Mrs. Beggs would some of the children come and do messages for them? Now we would have went for those messages, and my mother would have said, "Now, don't you take any money." That was the sort of a mother we had. We had to do the things, but we weren't to take money for doing it.

My young sister who was five years younger than me was the last to marry. I never had any family, but Myrtle and my other sisters and brothers, they all had. About two years later, her baby was born. But somehow or other she never seemed very well, and my mother kept saying, "I don't think Myrtle's very well." And we realised it ourselves. Finally she had to go to the doctor, and the doctor then referred her to the hospital. She was diagnosed as having hepatitis of the liver. Her own doctor told her husband that it was only a matter of six months. She didn't even get six months - she only got three months, and just after Christmas, January 1967, Myrtle died. This was a terrible heartache in our family, for she was the youngest. The baby then was about eight months old, and her husband's mother insisted on bringing up the little girl. We were happy enough at that, because it was his mother.

My mother never accepted that Myrtle had died, and just one year later she herself died. She had been out on the Saturday. There had been a lot of trouble on the Springfield Road that day between the Orangemen and republicans, and one man had been killed. He had got a brick threw at him, and he had died. When she came home, she was so upset and annoyed, and she began to be very sick. My father decided to send for the doctor. By the time I arrived, the doctor felt that it was her circulation, but to keep her quiet. Well, he went away, and that night I decided I would stay with my mother for fear she would get a wee bit worse or maybe want to get up the next day. So I said, "Look I will stay tonight and we will see how you are tomorrow."

That night was one of the worst nights on the Crumlin Road, because the IRA by then were doing an awful lot of bombing and shooting. Then about three o'clock in the morning, my mother sort of stirred a bit, and I had said to her, "Will I make you a cup of tea?" And she just gave a big sigh, and she says to me, "There is my Myrtle," and she is looking up at the ceiling. And I says to her, "For goodness sake, Mummy, now don't be annoying yourself like that." But she gave a big sigh, and that was her - dead. So I think that that always hurt me, because there was no way we could have got a doctor that night. The trouble was so bad. We had to wait to the next day before we could get anybody to come out to say, "Your mother's dead."

The Troubles had got very bad. Tommy, my husband, and I lived in Lawnbrook Avenue which had become a peace line. There had been an army post at the bottom of our street, separating Catholics and Protestants, and many's a night you could have heard the shooting from Clonard Gardens up to this army post. You just had to be very careful - you just did not go out at night time. My sister and brother-in-law came down one night, and sadly it was my brother-in-law's new car, and the next thing was we heard this terrible, terrible breaking of glass and just got out in time to see a crowd running up from Clonard Gardens. They had broke every window in the car. So I got a bit annoyed at this, because the nights that we were hearing shooting, we were getting our windows broke, and so I went round to Clonard Gardens, and I spoke to Father Reid. Apparently that priest now had a terrible bad breakdown, and he apologised, and he said he was very sorry at the trouble that the people - Protestant people - were having at the bottom of Lawnbrook Avenue. So, he said he would do his best to try to control this. He said he would sign any form that my brother-in-law could claim for the damage done to the car.

Then my husband took ill. I could of sort of accepted the things the way they were happening, but he got himself so tensed up and was attending the doctor with his stomach, and there was one night he took this awful bleeding.

Tommy and Elsie's home in Longbrook Avenue for which they recieved £700.

He was rushed into hospital, and he had a bleeding ulcer, and he was quite ill for a while after that. Our own doctor said, "Look, if you don't get out of there and this ulcer returns, he could bleed to death." So, it wasn't easy, because we owned our own house, but nobody was interested in buying it, and slowly but surely, the people who had rented houses moved away. We went to the Housing Executive, and they said they would do their best.

In the meantime, I was off work this day, and the next thing we were all told to get out quickly, and we all had to go up the street. The IRA had left a bomb at the army post, and there was a terrible, terrible explosion. There was only one soldier in the post that day, and he was killed, so the whole army post was blown to bits. That was in the 1970s, the early part of the Troubles. We went to the Housing Executive and we asked about our house, and could we be housed somewhere else? They didn't give us much hope, because we had no family. They were trying to house so many other people who had actually left the area. The time came when they could offer us a house, and it was away in Antrim which was about 15 or 16 miles away.

We lived three doors from the army post, and the IRA were shooting down at the army post, night after night. Sometimes the front windows were put in or the next week the back ones. We were putting in new windows, because we had been told, you can't claim unless you have £100 worth of damage. One night I was ironing, and a brick came through the window and landed on the ironing board.

My husband was standing at the front door one night, and this man introduced himself as Inspector Lolly, Community Police. He wanted to know – had we any complaints? We brought him into our house and explained about the windows. He told us we should have kept our receipts, then took them down once we had paid out £100. Nobody had given us this information.

A long time after all this trouble, the Housing Executive offered us a house in Antrim. We had to negotiate with them about a price – shock! They offered us £500, take it or leave it. I went back to them three or four times, and they raised it to £700. That is all we got for our home. So we left Lawnbrook Avenue and went to live in Antrim.

Now when we got out to Antrim, it took us a lot of months before we discovered that this estate that we were living in, there never seemed to be any lights on in the morning. And then we discovered that all these people that were on that estate didn't work. They were just lying in bed. So that meant that we were the only ones paying rent, and the rent was pretty expensive then. So we had said we'll not buy another house after what had happened. But

Tommy stopped his work at half past four. I didn't stop my work till nearly half past six, so that meant that he had to sit around waiting on me every night. We said, "Right, we'll put our pride in our pocket," and we started to go around house hunting again. And it was very well that we did this, because at that time... this area here - North Belfast - had been having a lot of trouble as well. So actually the houses had lost their value, so we walked into this house for £8,000 which was really a lot of money then, but it was brilliant for us. Thank God we were very happy and contented here, but the next thing we knew, Tommy had to have a treble bypass heart operation. So he was quite ill then. Now he was in hospital last Christmas, and the Christmas before that had been for his heart operation.

I always thank God that my church means a lot to me on the Springfield Road, because when we got married, we lived beside Tommy's mother who had multiple sclerosis. Really she needed a lot of help, because she was bedridden. So I joined Springfield Road Methodist Church, and although I was working, I hadn't much input to the church. Then whenever I retired out of work, I became more and more involved. The whole area 'round by the church had been all Protestants. But slowly but surely, they pulled all the houses down. They re-housed the people, and then Roman Catholics came into that area. To be quite truthful, the people were decent enough. You couldn't have said nothing about the people that were living beside the church.

The church then realised that we had lost an awful lot of members who had moved away, because the area now was just going to be another battleground. They made this agreement - would the members of the church agree that we would let half of the church become a community area? It was a big decision for members of the church, because some of them did not want it. They thought that the church should have closed, and for me, I said, "Well, we have a Protestant school up the Springfield Road, and them children are all right," so it is sad to think that we as a church are going to say, "Right, you can do what you want. We are moving out of this area as well." So I think I would say there was a good lot more people put up their hands to say that we would keep the church open, and that is how the church got permission for to keep our church open but to become a community centre which is now called Forthspring.

I did get involved at the beginning, because what had happened was they started up a lunch club. Now the lunch club was for both sides to come in, and we took our turn at making soup, sausage rolls and cups of tea, and all we charged was 50 pence. And that I would think was away in 1990 which is nine or ten years ago. Thank God it has went very well, and they are all very, very nice ladies. So I do a lot of work as regards the lunch club. We still have a lot of [church] members who would not take any part of Forthspring - sadly. They don't want nothing to do with it.

Now, we had a speaker every Monday night, and one of the speakers who came to take our meeting was Mr. Dessie Frizzell who had the fish shop on the Shankill Road. Dessie was one of the most loveliest Christian men that I have ever met, and it was a terrible, terrible blow when we discovered that his shop was the one that these IRA men had walked into and left the box. My niece is married to Dessie's wife's nephew. Apparently the truth was that the mother and the young daughter were in the shop working. It was a Saturday, and the mother had said to the young girl - another lovely wee Christian girl, - "Look, go you down - get your messages, and then I'll go for mine when you come back." But a customer came in to the shop, and the young girl says, "Look, Mum, I'll serve the customer, and you go down and you get your bread, and then when you come back I'll go." So Mrs. Frizzell was actually in O'Hara's Bakery when they heard the unmerciful explosion, because there was no warning. And they all run out and when she got up, that was the sight that she had seen. It was the saddest, saddest time, because what I remember of Dessie Frizzell, he had went to America at one time. He had been to a very, very poor area, so he thought he would like to do something for these people, and he was a beautiful singer. So he made a lot of tapes, and we all bought the tapes. He actually, I think, collected £2000, which was a lot of money then, and he sent this money to America - lovely, lovely man.

One bomber was killed. The one that left it, he didn't get out quick enough. But the other one, he got away, although he done time. But the one who was killed, Gerry Adams was the one who was carrying his coffin on his shoulders - proud for to be carrying the coffin. I am being very honest... I wouldn't even watch Gerry Adams on that television. When I look at him I think of Dessie, and if he had of realised the lovely Christian person... and the one that put the bomb to bomb that man - probably didn't mean to [kill him]. They said that it was some UFF had a room a wee bit further up and that was it. [They had gone to the wrong shop.]

As I say, other members of our church who had relatives... some of them policemen... blew to bits, living in fear of their lives, having to examine their cars every morning coming out, so they just don't want to be involved as regards anything in Forthspring or to be connected with it. You can do nothing about that. People have their own right to think whatever they want.

We have a church service every Sunday morning from 11 o'clock to 12.

Lately we have young boys kicking the door and wanting into the youth club which does not open on Sundays. A few Sundays ago, the door kept knocking and banging. One man from the church service went out. This man [standing outside the church] said he was sorry, but he had to chase two young lads out of the church grounds. They were trying to break into cars. The man's name was Paddy Maxwell – a very good man who worked with me in Marks and Spencer's. Paddy said, "I know Elsie Kirkpatrick, and this is her church. So I saw what these young lads were doing, and I chased them away." Paddy said the boys ran across the road which is the Catholic side. This has put a lot of people off in the church, and we have different episodes of these boys at night time trying to force their way in.

The church was burnt twice. Now that new minister - the Reverend David Canton - the first time I met him was the church had been burnt. Of course that meant everybody down to see what they could do to clean the church up. He was there with his t-shirt on him, and we all arrived with our buckets and cloths. The big hall got very badly burnt. The upstairs Forthspring was very badly burnt, but funny enough the church didn't get really badly burnt. It certainly needed a lot of cleaning. [There was a velvet cloth in the church] and on this velvet cloth there is a cross which was crocheted by a lovely lady out of our church who has since died. So this cross was sewn on to this velvet piece of material. And when that fire started, the cloth was burnt to a cinder, but the cross was not touched, and the cross is framed and it is hanging in the vestry. There was nothing left of that velvet cloth, but the wee small cross was lying...

I see an awful lot of good people within the Catholic community. I would say some of our Protestant women wouldn't come up to their standard as regards kindness, generosity and friendliness. Now I will give you an example - one of the ladies that I worked with in Marks and Spencer's is very good with floral arrangements. So I do the flowers in the church, and I happened to be talking to this lady one day and I says, "Oh, honest to goodness, I am beginning to panic, because this church is about to open [after the renovations to add the community centre], and everybody is sort of taking it for granted that I am going to be doing these flowers, and there is such a lot of people coming." I am beginning to say, "Oh dear, I am going to have to get somebody else to do these flowers." I didn't have to ask her - she says to me, "I'll do them," and she was a Catholic. And she not only done it, her husband and her brought all these flowers. I had wanted a stand in one corner for the flowers and then a big table arrangement on the communion table. She had went to the wholesale, her and her husband, and they brought all that stuff for me. They gave me the receipt.

And she did two beautiful, beautiful arrangements. They were magnificent. Some of the people were saying, "Elsie, the flowers are gorgeous," and I had to say, "Well, I am sorry, I didn't do them." But I did say who had done the arrangements, and I told the minister, and he asked if I would get a letter of thanks to them for what they had done.

I worked with them [Catholics] in the mill [as a teenagers]. But with working in Marks and Spencer's - we still have a Marks and Spencer's Retired Staff Association, and we meet once a month. I still am in contact with quite a lot of them. Some of them has died, and if it was a case of going up to the chapel for their funeral, well that wouldn't bother me at all. And I would be quite friendly with some of their husbands. If I would ring, and it would be their husbands there, "Well Elsie, how are you doing?" and a real, real friendliness really.

Now you were in your work from eight o'clock in the morning till six o'clock at night, and you just walked it home. You walked it to work, and you walked it home. The wages weren't what you call great. I had one friend, Maura Fern. Now Maura was the oddest girl that you could have wanted to know. She just did not mix with anybody. And I got on very, very well with her. We used to say to her, "Where is your mother today?" "My mother is away to chapel." And we used to have a great laugh. We used to say to her, "Your mother must have the chapel rails round her neck!"

Well, I would say now she probably then had republican ideas. But she would have came round to our house in Lawnbrook Avenue every Monday night. She lived in Clonard Gardens. She would have went up Clonard Gardens to get home. Now there was some Catholics standing one night, and Tommy had to come back home. They would have knew that was the Protestant area. Maura began to get worried in case somebody would have realised that he was a Protestant or could have been maybe one of the soldiers, and she stopped coming then. But she had came to our house for years, and the Troubles all stopped that. And I would send her a Christmas card every year - get a Christmas card from her - but even from the Troubles have stopped now, I never got on a friendly side of her. That friendship never started up again.

It is quite peaceful where we are living now, and you don't have any trouble - good neighbours. But it is a very changing world and a lot of sadness, a lot of hatred, a lot of badness. [The Troubles aren't over.] No, very, very sadly, no. We have always sort of said, "Once these Troubles would stop, it would take a long time for peace to come – so much hatred between Protestants and Catholics." Also the paramilitaries have now changed to drugs, drink and robbery.

I think most churches are suffering now, because younger people don't want church. Catholic people would tell you it is the same with them. They are finding it very hard for the younger people to accept what they are being taught. So this is where you will see all this badness I sort of feel. They are not being taught. There is no respect any more really.

I was a volunteer in the Northern Ireland Hospice and working in there and seeing these patients, you get to know these people. At the end of their day, let them be Catholics or Protestants, they just die the same way. So to me, I just say, "Whether you are Catholic or Protestant, whether you are black or white, Jew or whatever, it is the man above who judges how you have lived." That is my attitude to life, and I don't judge anybody. I live my life and do the best that I can. I thank God every day for health to be able to do what I do and for my family, and I love my church.

Patrick

Patrick O'Connor whose pen name is Padraic Fiacc is known as "the Troubles Poet." Close friends call him, "Joe." His formative years were spent in New York City where he was confronted with multi-culturism and racial injustice. This exposure influenced his attitudes and his poetry. He now lives in Belfast.

My name is Patrick Joseph O'Connor, and my pen name is Padraic Fiacc. I was born in 1924 when the Irish Civil War was just petering out and the new state of Northern Ireland was just born. My father had to get out of the country, because he was IRA, and my mother, two brothers and I stayed at home. My mother didn't want to go to America. She was told to go there, to leave her own country, but she was a mad rebel.

I was the first born alive, and I was very close to my mother, but I didn't really know her as a child. I was left with my grandmother whose head went away, because she was burned out of her home in Lisburn and had to go to East Street in the Markets. I was left with the grandmother, and I overheard my aunt calling her a nasty woman. So I always thought of her as "the nasty woman." And the poor woman, I mean, she really was suffering. She lost everything, and it was a come down to have to live in a kitchen house in the Markets. My mother and us kids were living with her. She wasn't able to cope. She wanted my mother to go to America to her husband who lived there.

My mother was a flapper in those days - she loved style. All the mill girls loved style, and they'd get dressed up on Sundays. Dad sent her money regularly, hoping that she would come after him to America. He sent her more money, and she went out and bought a red leather raincoat, and she came home with it. My grandmother went mad. She took a hold of it - I was a witness to it - this was dinnertime. They threw plates at each other, and I was holding onto Aunt Mary. Aunt Mary said to the two of them, "Don't forget there's children in this room," but that didn't stop it. The grandmother got one end of the raincoat, and Mother had the other end. It was a tug-of-war, but you couldn't tear a leather raincoat apart - I mean the coat was saved anyway. She was telling the factory girls that she worked with about the whole thing, and they said, "He'll run off with another woman, if you don't go back to him." She said, " I don't care. I wish he would." One of the girls she worked with said, "Did you ever bet on a horse?" And she said, "No." "Bet on a horse. Maybe you'll get a lot of money," and she did. She got 90 pounds which was a lot in those days - in the 20s. And it got us second–class on the boat to America, because she was very proud. She wasn't gonna go steerage which the Irish people had to - in the hold of the ship.

[Feeling at home in Belfast] goes back to childhood, and our mother didn't want to go to America. My brother, Brian, was a year younger than me, and when we were going up the gangplank to the boat, he and I went first. Our mother was carrying Rory. Brian stopped in the middle of the gangplank, and he said, "I don't wanna go to America." And he said, "I wanna go back to me da on the cobbles," and I said, "Brian, he's not your da - he's your grandfather. " I was trying to be adult and all - but I didn't want to go to America either. I said, "You're going to meet your real father, your real da." My mother had to yell at him to move.

So we arrived in America, but my father wasn't there to meet us. He took the wrong train! I had an uncle with a cab, and he met us, and he brought us home. Dad had a lovely apartment on 96th Street - on the west side – a beautiful apartment, and well, as a child, I didn't really know what was happening. [Patrick went to various American schools and saw racial prejudice firsthand. He never lost his desire to return to Northern Ireland.]

I took this Swedish boat, the Grisholm, back to Ireland. I was only turned 20 or so. I was going through all kinds of paranoia until I got onto the boat itself. It was known in Europe for helping refugees to get to Portugal or some neutral country. They were afraid of the mines in the Atlantic, and so they took a different route to Ireland. It took us nine days to get there. There was a French colony on it and Irish people, but the French never came to deck drill. They were always complaining. I took a turn against America, but I took a worse turn against the French!

There was a fellow from Belfast in our cabin, and he was carrying on. There were other people in our cabin, but they were from the south of Ireland. This Belfast guy was carrying on, "Why is it taking so long?" And I said, "Because it you don't want your arse blown off, there's mines in the water." He annoyed me. He gurned and yapped all night to the end of the voyage. And there was an old man from the west of Ireland, and I saw the difference between the Ulster person and the persons from the south of Ireland. I didn't have anything to do with it - it was just different personalities.

[Speaking about the differences in the north and south of Ireland] Well, [in the north] they're politically orientated and they're both the same religion – Christianity. They're Christian, but because of the historical context, they're really one people. You can tell by listening to their voices. They have a different temperament from the people of the south of Ireland. Maybe they're more forthright and straightforward. They talk a lot and talk quicker than they think. There's something amusing about it – of course it's not amusing now. Actually, to me, it's a family feud that's going on now, and if there's anything more devastating than a family feud...if you read their writers, for instance, they have a different slant to the writers in the south of Ireland. The Catholics in the north are more like the Protestants than they are like the Catholics from the south, and their form of Christianity - they take religion very seriously, and unfortunately they use it as a weapon. The Protestant Reformation is very strong today in Northern Ireland, almost more so than it was when it was first created by Martin Luther.

What's happening today is that they're becoming part of Europe, and religion itself is coming together more - the Protestant and Catholic. For instance, Rome salutes Martin Luther now. They see a whole lot of good in him, and the Anglican religion, for instance, or the Church of Ireland, are really Catholic as far as theology goes. I think it's sad that they fight with one another, because they're obviously just using what they have - and what you have, you hold. That's the motto here, but it's going bad on them. It's going bad on the people of Northern Ireland, because they're being represented abroad as stubborn thick heads. Nobody understands the situation, because we ourselves don't understand it. It's sad, because they're good people - both sides are good. They're good people, and they're hard workers. What's happening here is so completely uncharacteristic of them, because they're a genteel people at heart. The military thing... well I'm not a great lover of the military, but it spoils everything. Now when I came over in the 40s, we were able to laugh at each other and make fun of each other and laugh at ourselves. Joseph Tomelty wrote plays that were put on in the Group in which he made fun of the Catholics and the Protestants being orange and green. That was a healthy thing in those days.

It's not a joke now though - you can't even turn it into a joke. There's too much tension, and too many people have died. It's still lingering on inside us, and it's not good for mental health. It's the lingering on bit – the victims. I wouldn't comment as a victim, but I really am a victim, because it changed my whole life and shot my nerves.

Well, I think, I have hope, because the Catholic is unionist just as well as Protestant is unionist, because we want a united Ireland, and the Protestants want a united Britain and Ireland. Actually we are united geographically, and now that we're in the European block, a lot of this nonsense is going to have to go, especially when it's ending in murder and terrible intimidation, not to mention mental torture.

Oh, in the meantime I had renounced my American citizenship because of my passport. You see I wanted to be Irish, so I had to renounce my American citizenship. There was a woman counsel at the time who said, "My dear boy, nobody, but nobody, renounces their American citizenship." Well I said, "I am somebody," and I said, "What about Charlie Chaplin and Greta Garbo?" "My dear boy, you're not Greta Garbo - you're not Charlie Chaplin. I want you to go home and think about it, but personally, I think you're tied to your mother's apron strings."

And they were publishing my poems in Dublin, the ones about the Troubles. So I got to be known as the "Troubles Poet," and there was a furore going on – the idea that a poet should write about anything political. They never mentioned their politics, but I had a deeper idea of that. I was looking at Canadian television that was brought over here, and the poets from Belfast were over there, and I wasn't invited. They were all reciting poems about love and the shrubbery, and age and all like that – not a word about the Troubles. And the Canadian interviewer said, "Such beautiful cadences from such a troubled place."

In the meantime, I edited this anthology ["The Wearing of the Black"], and it was published by Blackstaff, and it caused a furore. The poets in the south were yelling, "There's no war. What are you talking about? There's no war." They didn't know how bad it was up here, but everybody [in the anthology] wrote about the Troubles. This young fella who I knew as a boy used to bring me his boyhood poems - came to visit me when Nancy [Patrick's ex-wife] left. And he was working in a factory, and he used to come every Saturday and bring beer, fish and chips. He was so humorous. I used to like to talk to him. He wrote poetry, and I said, "I'm putting one of your poems in the anthology, but I want you to change your name – like me, have a pen name." So he was called Gerry McLoughlin, so I said, "Say Gerry Locke," so he changed his name. I put him in the anthology.

So Gerry McLoughlin, the wee fella, said that he would get his tape recorder from his sister. His sister had one, and he wanted to record it [a broadcast by Patrick], so he came that Sunday. I hate my voice on radio - I really don't like it. But he came, and the recorder didn't work, and he kept on fumbling at it. And I said, "Gerry, take that bloody thing and throw it out the window - it's not working." I said, "I don't want to hear the broadcast anyway."

So he just jumped on me and knocked me to the floor and was like strangling me. It was so unlike himself. I was on the floor and said, "You could have choked me. What the hell is wrong with you?" And then he told me. He said that every Sunday that he came to my house, he was being followed by men in a car. There's a name for it - it's called fingering. They let you know that they are going to kill you. I said, "Gerry, bullets don't grow on trees." And I tried to turn it into a joke. I said, "You're leading a Walter Mitty life - who the hell would want to kill you?"

He was becoming a foreman. He was the only Catholic in a Protestant factory. So it was the weekend. I said, "All right. Do you remember the car and the people in it?" And I said, "Write down a description of the car," (I gave him a piece of paper.) and he knew the license plate and all. And he described the men in the car. I was suffering from the break-up with Nancy, and my nerves were bad.

Then he wrote down the list of the people, and that was frightening. So I told the other poets, and they said, "Joe, you can't take responsibility, because you're not able to make decisions right now." They said, "Go to his father, or go to the police." So when he came back, I said, " They told me to go to your father, or go to the police, " and he said, "If you go to the police, you'll be signing my death warrant. If you go to my father, he'll send me out of the country, and he needs my money." He was the oldest of a big family. So we went on and on, and I hemmed and hawed, and they said, "Bring him out to the garden, and he can help you with the garden."

So one day I brought him out to the garden, and I said, "I'll cut the grass, and you can do the weeding," and he said, "No, I'll cut the grass, and you can do the weeding!" I started to weed the buttercups from the carnations - buttercups are like a weed. But he had the three lawns cut, just like that. I said, "Come on, Gerry, into the house and we'll have a talk." And I said, "Lie down on the studio couch and make believe I'm a psychiatrist. Tell me what's really eating you." He said, "This issue of closing the high school – I could have finished the high school." (It was a Catholic high school in a Protestant community.) He said, " I want to go to university." "Well," I said, "why don't you go to the Open University and still become the foreman in the factory?" So I talked to him about the Open University. A lot of people did that. They did their day's work and studied at night. And matter of fact, a poet friend of mine did that, and he got a wonderful job. I talked him into it, and then I was exhausted.

He was going home that night, and I said, "Now don't you come back and depress me." They killed him that morning. Protestant guys in the factory were calling him the "fenian bastard" or "fenian get." He said, "I'm going to report

you to the manager." And I don't know whether he reported them or not, but he was very fierce. My "Odour of Blood" was in the libraries, and there was a picture of me on the back of it. He said, "Joe you shouldn't have put a picture of you on the back of that." He was worried about me.

There was one day when he was visiting me. His fingernails were very long on his right hand, and I said, "Why don't you cut your fingernails? That's awful ugly looking. Why are you letting them grow like that?" And he said, " If they shoot me, I'll dig my fingernails into the other hand. I'll take the pain to the other hand." And his hands were clawed like that after his murder. He was buying cigarettes for his girlfriend, and they were going to work. She thought his killers were thieves, and she took her purse to give it to them. And she handed it, but they just shot him – six times.

This boy that they murdered – well he was a boy to me – he was only turned 20, and he had everything to look forward to in life, and I was trying to get him to finish his education. But he was so humorous, such an uplifting person, you know. I couldn't even think of it happening. I just got up one morning and turned the radio on. It was cricket, and I listened to the third program for the music, and it was cricket. I hate sports, so I switched it to Radio Ulster, and then a young fellow was found shot - Carnmoney district - and I knew that when they said Carnmoney, that's where his factory was. Talk about being silenced...I tried not to believe I was paranoid. That's the thing I accused Gerry of being. And then I couldn't do anything, and there was a bottle of Italian Cinzano Bianco in the fridge. I took it out, and I poured myself a drink and sat down.

And then there came a knock at the door, and it was the sexton's wife. They knew me, and they read my poetry books. And they had an Alsatian – a neutered Alsatian dog – and I knew her by the dog, and she said, "Joe, I just wanted to come and tell you in case you heard it accidently." Then I sat down, and I knew then. I actually thought I saw him. He said, "Joe, Joe, be good, be good." When the sexton's wife left me, I drank the whole bottle of Cinzano Bianco, and I threw it against Nancy's books.

I blamed myself, but the cops said they would have got him anyway. Now they said, "Don't blame yourself." "Well," I said, "I should have gone to you guys, or I should have gone to his father." He was so much against going to the cops and so much against going to his father that I didn't know what the hell to do, and I couldn't make decisions at that time.

[Out of this painful death, emerged the poem, 'The Ditch of Dawn, A Requin For Gerry McLaughlin, Murdered 7 April 1975'.]

How I admired your bravado
Dandering down the road alone
In the dark yelling, 'I'll see
You again tomorrow' but
They pump six bullets into you.
Now you are lying in a mud
Puddle of blood, yelling
'There is no goodbye'
No safe home'
In this coffin country where
Your hands are clawed...

How can I tell anyone
I'm born, born lying in
This ditch of a cold
Belfast dawn
With the bullet-mangled
body of
A dead boy
And can't,
Can't get away?
A young
Brit soldier wanders
Over to my old
donkey honk
Of bitter miserere of
Dereliction on the street.
'What is it mate, what is it?
WHAT'S WRONG?'

I was walking down the street one day, and the soldiers were searching people. And this kind of crazy soldier came over to me, and he snatched "Odour of Blood" out of my hand. He opened it up and read, "Go home, you British bastards, for we are more British than you." Oh, he took exception to that. He said, "Did you write this?" "Well," I said, "look at the picture on the back of it, and tell me if it's me." He started to persecute me, and every time I passed, he made me stand up against the wall and be searched. I couldn't even go into town to the library. He seemed to be everywhere. So Paddy Devlin lived across the street, and I went over to him, and I told him the situation. And he said, "You are going to report that fella to the police." And I said, "Paddy, I'm in Andersonstown. If I got caught going into the barracks - the police barracks." "Well," he said, "If you don't do it, I will." So he lifted the phone and said, "This person is a very distinguished poet."

So I waited, but the soldier still was annoying me. Paddy Devlin called the police, and I had to make a formal complaint. Paddy made me. He got it from the police station, but I had to sign it. I was so appreciative at that time. It was bad in the 70s. It gave me an insight into what could happen to anybody. I wasn't following the emergency acts, but I was right in the middle of it all. For some of us, it was a reign of terror, because of the seemingly random behaviour of the paramilitaries. But it wasn't random. It was tit-for-tat after a while, and nobody was spared – an old woman, children. It was really war crimes. We tried not to recognise that it was a war, but it was a war. And it lasted for so long – three decades. Well, they successfully terrorized me. I was in a state of terror many's a time. And I actually took the fire poker to bed with me and a knife and hammer and scissors and actually dreamed of killing someone who would come in.

Gerry Adams asked me to judge some poems of the prisoners, and I would award the prisoners. And we all went to the Falls Road Library to go over the poems and read some of them and pick the best ones. And Gerry said to me, he said, "Joe, we've got to get our arses out of here." He said, "There's a book bomb." It was a library. It was a book bomb. So we all went down to what you call "The Mill." It's an old mill in Belfast, but they converted it into a kind of school – a school for adults going into creative writing. So we all went in where I got a drink. It's sad, you see. Even the good things that you try to do are frustrated in one way or the other.

An IRA prisoner came to me one day and said, " Why do you write about and praise the soldiers?" I said – a whole lot of people had asked me that question. Well, why I really did it was I had younger brothers in the services in America. I used to worry about them in different countries that they were in. As the oldest brother, I used to write about them. And when I see these young Brit fellas - it's just a job to them. I actually was going to go into the army in America, but my kid brother, Jimmy, who was in it – was something high up in the army – he says, "Don't go into the army." I was looking for a job - the problem is, it's a job. The people really go into things like that, because they need the money.

You see, you can't associate all the Protestants with the paramilitaries. They might sympathize, but they wouldn't go to the length that the paramilitaries have gone. I have a poem, and it's been severely criticized, of course. Criticism's good - I'm making people think. This young poet from the south of Ireland wrote and said – he was horrified that I wrote all that in the open, especially in poetry. He wrote, "There is no war, and we poets do not write our poems out on the street." You know, he went on and on with it, and I was going to quote him, because it was so revealing of how little was the concern for us in the north. I was going to quote him, but he asked me not to, because he realized, I think, that things weren't as casual... and he said, "They're just a bunch of gangsters." They were idealistic kids in their twenties when they went off to some organisation or the other. They really believed in what they were doing. The Catholics believed that they were uniting Ireland, and the Protestants believed that they were defending their own culture.

Some young men went on a hunger strike, and Thatcher could have stopped it, but she hadn't the vaguest idea about Ireland. To this day – I don't want to knock her too much – but I understood them all. I understood why they were doing the things they do. Of course the obvious thing was violence wasn't the way to do it. I'm a pacifist, and I don't think there is a military solution, and in one of my poems, my mother is talking to me and she says – "You're still a soldier - it's only that you're losing the war, and all the wars are lost anyway." She was a fighter, but she didn't believe in the military. And then, you see, the police were identified with the military, because they were highly armed, and they were a Protestant force. And then that's why the fella they murdered wouldn't let me go to them.

One night I went up to Andersonstown. I lived up there. And I was walking with a friend to his house, and then I walked back. A gang of these fellas I had seen before were sitting on a rail and trying to listen to my conversation with a Dutch girl who was interested in my poems. They ran after me, and I said, "They're not running after you, they're just running. They have to do something." And I said, "Don't give in to this paranoia." I paused under a dark tree, and I had these glasses that a publisher gave me – silver rims - and the lenses would turn dark in the light. They were a prized possession which I really enjoyed wearing, but they went for the glasses, of course. They pulled them off and jumped on them. Well, I already knew the two things they didn't want were light or noise. When I get angry, I can really yell. So they really were going to kill me... and I wasn't a spring chicken even then... and so they kicked my head and everything. They were going to kick me to death. I started yelling. It frightened the shit out of them. I didn't come from tough New York to take this kind of goo.

Then I went home to the landlady. She had white carpets and a white poodle, and every time you would go to use the phone, the poodle would jump up onto the phone. She worshiped this poodle, and I was bleeding something terrible – from top to toe. I was spilling blood all over her white carpet, and she never said a word. She never said, " What happened to you, Joe?" I said, "May I use your telephone?" And she said, "Yes," and then the bloody poodle jumped up...it's the little things in life that you remember. And I phoned for a friend to come and bring me to their house - he lived nearby - and the first thing he said was, "Jesus, Joe."

When I went to the doctor, I said, "I think you'll have to strap my ribs." And he said, "We don't do that anymore." (I was kicked in the ribs, and I thought I had broken ribs, because a pain was there). He said, "What happened to you?" And I said, "I was beat up." "But why were you beat up?" He knew damn well. He pulled the shutters down - that was the way it was. Sure I was afraid to go to the police. I had no redress whatsoever. I had learned my lesson, because that was cold Falls Road. You really were censored by unseen people, and they had successfully terrorized us into silence. That's why I was so outspoken, because I couldn't stay in that kind of chicken coop. One good thing about New York was it was noisy. A lot of New York comes out in me here. I'm more broad-minded. They don't know whether to call me an Irish poet, a British poet, or an American poet. So I just say, " Just call me Poet."

It makes me angry [when people say they haven't been touched by the Troubles]. I don't know why, but it's a trait of the Irish people and I've found it's an English trait too. The Welsh have it too, but the Scottish don't. They're whiskey drinkers! Maybe the whiskey uninhibits you. No, the English have it too, very strong. And when the Troubles started here, it was just nothing to them. They didn't want to know. They had enough on their plate without those Paddy Irish.

I don't know how I got through those years, because everything was happening at once. One trouble seemed worse than another. That's why I find it so difficult to write an autobiography. Some of it still is entangled in such a complex way that it's like a nest of entangled snakes.

Jean

Jean lives in a nursing home in east Belfast where she has lived all her life. She has a deep Christian faith. She was 80 years old when this interview was recorded.

I was born on a wee street called Ardlawn Street. And then I moved...it would have been in east Belfast. I've lived all my life here in east Belfast.

I was born in 1919. I get mixed up in the year I was born and the year I was saved sometimes. It's 1919. I'm 80 years old. It was 1929 when I accepted the Lord as my Saviour. It was three weeks before my tenth birthday, and I couldn't live any other life, only for the Lord. And people think maybe if you're a Christian, life's dull - but it's not. It's not.

And I remember one time I was in deep, deep distress, and I was down on my knees praying. My father's mind went, and he went to Purdysburn. That nearly broke my heart, you know. You can understand that. And I remember being down on my knees, praying, and the arms folded around me. And some people smiled at that, but it was true, because Scripture says, "In and around about are the everlasting arms." Like, I know my Bible. I've read it through. You just couldn't repeat it all, but things happen - it comes to you, you know.

Well I've only one brother and no sisters. Mommy had a wee girl two years before me, but she was only an "eight months' birth," and she only lived an hour. Many's the time I wish she had lived. But my brother and I have never fell out in our lives – never fought. And when we were children, if one got hit, two cried. My father and mother's both away home to be with the Lord years ago.

I went to a wee school in Comber Street. I went to a wee school, and then they built all the new schools. I went to seventh standard. I was in public high school, you know. We were just like other children – you just played in the street and all. But there was one thing we didn't do, my brother and I - that was disobey our parents, for they wouldn't have it which was right. They taught us the truth, but they never were hard on us. You know, they weren't hard on us. Like if we needed a smack, we got it, but it wasn't half killing us.

I went to a wee mission hall called Foundry Street. Well, I go to the Church of God now. In fact when I came in here, my brother said, "You make that church your place of worship."

When I was working, I worked in a wareroom at first, you know, where they make clothes now. And then after that I worked in munitions – during the war like, you had to go and work. And I started in the night shift. You did a week of night shift and then a week on the day shift, and I started on night shift. I worked making clothes, but then when the war broke out I had to work in munitions. Like you had to go into munitions to help your country.

And I was only in a very short time, when a girl came over to me, and she said, "Are you a Christian?" I says, "Yes." And she says, "I knew it the moment I looked at you." So we must have a look of our own. That's the one thing the Lord has blessed me with – was contentment. If you're not content, you're only interested in yourself maybe. But the most of my family circle are born again people.

You see I never was married. I was out with a couple of boys, but it was never anything. And I remember in work this man coaxed me, he says, "I will go to church with ya." I says, " I know," but I says, "No, it's not the thing." But he came to me awhile after that too. I remember this as well, and he says, "I just came, Jean, to tell ya - I accepted the Lord as my Saviour." And I said, "Oh, I'm delighted to hear that." Now I wouldn't despise unsaved people. No, I wouldn't. They can't help that they haven't been told the truth. It's not their fault.

After the war – I was ready for retirement then. Oh, it's a good while now. I'm 80 now. In fact, I asked for early retirement, for at that time Mother was still living. And I knew she couldn't look after herself, and she had a lot of falls. I was worried about her, you know. And I just asked for the early retirement, and I never wanted for anything since it. My father could look after himself, but he lost his memory in the end. And I tried to help him all I could, but I looked well after Mother, and I kept her clean and got her lovely clothes and give her good food and all. And I gave my father good food too. Yes, I looked after them in their later years, looked well after them. And when people came into our house, they knew they was getting a cup of tea. And I went into the kitchen to make it, and they used to say that my mother's eyes stayed on that door 'til I walked out again. She just wanted me all the time, you know. And so one woman said to me, "She's selfish." I says, "No. My mother never was selfish." Neither was my father. They always put my brother and I first, and so they did. But when she got older like, she couldn't do for herself, and I looked after her. And that's what made her watch the door, you know.

Now my father died before my mother. Well sure my mother died on the Twelfth Day, and I thought there would be nobody at the funeral hardly. It was the biggest funeral down the street, 'cause the people were coming up from the Bridge Road after seeing the Orangemen and stopped at the corner when they

DONEGALL SQUARE BELFAST No. 77

saw the funeral, you know.

Well, you see, if my father and mother didn't agree on things, it was never in front of my brother and I. It was true... during the day you was out in the street playing, and at night we were in bed. They never disagreed in front of us. We never fought with the neighbours or anything. And when we were children, if we went in with a complaint, my mother would have said, "If you can't agree, come in. I'm not going on the street to argue about this." And that's sensible. Now I remember this person... I think it was my aunt and some of the rest of them, and they were arguing over children. The ones they were arguing about was dancing around the street and their arms around each other. The children don't hold spite. Sure they don't - children don't hold spite.

I remember the bombing of Belfast during World War II. It was terrible. You were in the dark. You didn't put the lights on at night or anything. You were in the dark, and sometimes you'd lie on the floor instead of lying on the bed to escape it, you know. And I can't remember an awful lot about it, but nothing happened to our family circle, you know.

You prayed that the Lord would protect you. You see, I have great faith in prayer. Some people don't. See some people say... if they don't get what they want... what they prayed for – they think the Lord didn't answer their prayer. But that's wrong, because sometimes the Lord says, "No. It's not the right thing for you." And that's sensible to think that way.

Well see, the Lord doesn't give you everything you want. He gives you everything that's good for you. He'll not give you everything you want. I have a poem right here that says my life's in the Lord's hands. He knew best. I just rested in the Lord's hands. He looked after me. I have great faith in the Lord.

[Speaking of the Troubles] I know it was awful. We had sympathy with them, no matter whether they were Roman Catholics or Protestants. At least, when you're a Christian, I believe you show sympathy with them. And there's Roman Catholics in our family. Like I had a cousin married one, you know. But he told us he would never put his foot in the chapel again. He kept his word like. He did keep his word, and he started to go to a church with her. And there was a big tent mission on one time, and they were coming from all churches to it. And when the appeal was made, he got up and walked up in front of everybody and accepted the Lord as his Saviour.

You don't despise them. They can't help what they're born into - wouldn't matter to me whether they're Roman Catholic or Protestant. The Lord died for them too. They need to be born again too. And when they do, you'll find that they make great Christians. They've proved that.

Like there's one thing I wouldn't be hard on Roman Catholics. I remember one time, it was at the blitz, and there were awful riots. It was terrible. And somebody said to me about the Roman Catholics. I says, "Well, the Lord died for them as much as He died for the Protestants." And it wouldn't be in my place to be hard on them. And you find if they do accept the Lord as their Saviour, they become great Christians. They live the life. You see, I'm a contented sort of person – and just whatever the Lord has for me, pleases me all right. I know God's way of salvation with having born again parents. And we used to have family worship. Scripture says, "Godliness with contentment is great gain." You see, I've been blessed with contentment.

Another girl who's a Christian come up where I was shopping, and the girl says, "Jean, she wants to tell you something." And I had an idea then what it was. I says, "What is it?" And she says, "I got saved. I accepted the Lord last night." I says, "Then you're my sister in the Lord." Everybody needs God's salvation. And they think, you see, whenever you're a Christian, you're dull. No sort... you have a contented mind.

I'm happy enough here... and I read a lot. I do read a lot. But I read other things as well as my Bible like, but now my brother buys me clean books. You couldn't say anything about them, you know. He buys me a Telegraph too. I'm four years older than him – four years and one day. And we're best of friends – never fought.

Lillian

Lillian McArdle was born in Dublin but has lived most of her life in Northern Ireland. She was educated at Queens in the 1930s and was a schoolteacher most of her working life. She speaks about what it was like to rear sons in Belfast.

I was born, believe it or not, in Dublin – 1918 during the "Black Flu." Then the family came back to Belfast, except I do remember we often went to Dublin for holidays. During one of these holidays, the Four Courts were blown up, probably around 1922. We went to get away from the troubles – nothing changes here. My father and mother had taken a house in Sandymount, and Daddy stayed in town.

I also remember Michael Collins' funeral. On one side of the bridge over the Liffey, one found mostly hotels and on the other very high buildings. In one of these buildings my father hired a high window – rather like they do nowadays for coronations and events. And I remember being at the window. My father and mother were there and several other people too, simply and solely to see Collins' funeral. And all I remember is… I was bored out of my skull, I suppose… there must have been hundreds and thousands of people on each side of the bridge and the funeral cortége passing. I would have been about four or five.

I remember another incident about the same time which is still a mystery to me and which I would like an historian to solve for me. We were still in Sandymount, which was always very quiet and had four roads running out of it like spokes of a wheel. I used to be allowed to go up to the shop, because I didn't have to cross a road. And I remember going up one day, and it must have been summer. It was sunny, and I was going up to the shop, and suddenly there was nobody there but me. And down what must have been the Dublin Road came this huge lorry filled with men in uniform – with guns. Of course I thought this was exciting, and they turned down one of the side roads, stopping at the first house. The men jumped off the lorry, and some of them ran up the steps to the front door, while some of them hammered at the basement door. My mother must have heard something and raced up to grab me, terrified. And I never found out which forces they were. They certainly weren't the Black and Tans. But whether they were Treaty or opposition forces, I know not. Infuriating, isn't it? [The incident] was never mentioned. I think Mama was absolutely horrified that I'd been caught in it at all. She had thought it was safe to go up to the local shop. Nobody would have thought…

My father was a publican. He used to say that he had at one time or another owned every public shop in Belfast, not all at the one time of course. And one of his earlier stories of the Troubles, and I think it's a pity that it's not repeated more often, is that his life was saved by a Protestant.

He owned a pub at what was then the foot of the Crumlin Road, and it was called the "Glenview." And he went in one Friday, and he had a Protestant barman, which was rare then. And the barman said to him, "You'll not be in on Friday, Mr. O'Neill." Daddy replied, "Of course I'll be in on Friday – it's the busiest day of the week." The barman replied, "Ah well, do you not remember saying you had something to do?" And Daddy thought, "Odd." So he didn't go in on Friday, and two boyos sat with guns the whole night waiting for him. So Daddy always swore that that Protestant barman saved his life. That must have been about 1924, I suppose.

I graduated from Queens in 1939, and I was bound and determined not to teach. No way was I going to teach. I mean, teaching jobs at that time were quite literally knocking at my door, and I didn't want any of them – pure prejudice.

But just that year the Postal and Telegraph Censorship opened here. Now that was a wartime thing. We were appointed from England, so it had nothing to do with Northern Ireland Civil Service. It was almost even Stephen – Catholic and Protestant - because there was no interest in England what we were. I must say I enjoyed the four years I worked in it. Oh, aye, it was great fun. There were a variety of jobs one could do, and I did sorting for awhile, but mostly you opened letters from England to people here – to avoid giving information to the enemy. The enemy, mind you, I think knew it far better than we did. And you cut out silly things like…"We had visitors all night last night." That was a no, no. In view of recent films, I sometimes wonder how effective it was. And so much was rather silly. To give an example: I remember getting two letters in the same pile… small brown envelopes… not the business kind. The first one was addressed to Miss Mary Jones [naturally, I don't remember the real names]. I opened it, and the letter began, "Dear Mum and Dad." I thought, "Oh, dear." And I opened the second addressed Mr. and Mrs. Brown to find, "Darling Mary." The poor, silly boy had put them in the wrong envelopes. But I wasn't allowed to touch them. I had to let them go. I've wondered what happened. From the tone of the letters, she was probably a friend of the family.

This is one of the craziest stories of the war. We were very badly bombed on Atlantic Avenue for two nights, although I don't know why we went on about our blitzes, when you think about places like Coventry that got it night after night after night. I don't know how they ever stood it. The second blitz was in April, and my father was just out of hospital after a hip operation. We used to get our taxis from O'Kanes who were funeral furnishers in Donegall Street. But I rang for a taxi to get my father and myself out of town. "Ah, Miss O'Neill, no chance, no taxi." They said all their taxis were out dealing with blitz casualties. "Well," I said, "I want a taxi." And finally… "Well… I'll tell you what. We'll get one. We'll take you as far as Glengormley." And I thought, "Right." All I wanted was to get into the taxi. So we got as far as Glengormley, and of course I wouldn't let the driver go. I must have been one of the original hijackers! And of course, he was only too glad to get a wee run out of town. So we went right down the coast. We eventually got to Glenarm and into a hotel on a side street. In fact, Glenarm was a side street! I'll never forget waking the next morning and hearing a cock crow.

But after that, I travelled every day from Glenarm to Belfast to the censorship offices. We couldn't live in Belfast any longer. My father was still on crutches, and fifteen people had died in Atlantic Avenue – a direct hit on an air-raid shelter.

The bus passed along the coast road - if it felt like it - about half six in the morning, and brought us into Larne and the train from Larne to Belfast. And then we took whatever conveyance we could get to the office. Then of course the censorship offices got a direct hit, and we had to move out to Drumglass House in the grounds of Victoria College.

Then my father and I moved from Glenarm to Portstewart and we stayed in a house we had stayed in sometimes for holidays – Mrs. Kerr's. I travelled from Portstewart then for another few years by bus and train. We were there at the time of Pearl Harbour, because that I remember vividly.

But anyway, when I was travelling up and down, I remember getting on the Portstewart train one evening, and these two lovely American boys got on. I was so old fashioned, you wouldn't encourage them, not however much you wanted to. They sat opposite me, you see, and they sort of tentatively smiled. No, I had the book up like that [demonstrates], and I must have been abominably prim and proper. There are no two ways about it. So they then enjoyed themselves you see. They weren't a bit rude, but they were making cracks you see, and still the book stayed up. So eventually the one lad, "Scuse me ma-am." And I said, "Yes?" It would have frozen an Eskimo! And he said, "Scuse me ma-am, but do you not know your book is upside down?" Which it

Belfast men working on bomb reconstruction in London during WWII.

was, so what do you do after that?

Several years later when my second son, John, was about six or seven, St. Brigid's School opened and I was approached. I thought I wouldn't like teaching, but by that time, I was very glad to be offered a job. And I took it, and I loved it - I loved it. And I miss it terribly at my age. I liked the girls - now not in any mushy way. I mean I murdered them. But, I must have done something right, because they still come to see me. I never played for popularity. And I never used a cane, as I consider that a form of violence. But they tell me I didn't have to use a cane, because they dreaded my tongue worse than the cane! The lovely thing about it is, they remember even that with affection. You know, one of them said, "My God, you were a holy terror." That's a compliment?

I said, "You always used to say I was an old villain." But the greatest compliment I think I ever got was when one of them said, "Yes, but you were always fair." No one could say anything that would please me better than that. And I enjoyed the young minds. I enjoyed the brushing together of minds, and I enjoyed them opening up. Oh that doesn't mean that there weren't times - I used to say it depends on what day you ask me whether I like teaching. If it was Monday, yes I liked teaching. If it was Friday - no, I can't get out quick enough.

I taught English and drama, and we put on quite a few musicals. Sister Cecilia was head of music. Oh, she was a pet. She was very musical, and she was only ever interested in the score. Oh, I really must have been an awful thorn in her flesh, as I was mainly interested in the acting. Once we were watching a rehearsal, and the choruses were going on and on, so I said, "Sister, this could go on all night." She replied, "But sure, it is lovely." So banking on my guess that she would not have read the words, I said, "Well O.K., Sister, if you don't mind our girls singing about having a tumble in the hay, I don't care." She nearly collapsed on the spot and babbled, "Oh dear, does it actually say that? We'll take that chorus out, girls."

She said to me, "Well what do you think, Lillian? What do you think?" I said, "Well, Sister, if you want an honest answer, I think it's bloody awful." So it was. And she said, "Ah, you're terrible. Ach, you're awful. You shouldn't say things like that." And I said, " Ach, I know, Sister. Sure you should know by now that I'm an old bitch anyway." After a long pause – "Well… yes you are, Lillian, but lovable with it!" Isn't that gorgeous? So I maintain that that has given me carte-blanche to be as bitchy as I like! So anyway, I taught there until I had to retire at 65.

And my first year of retirement was absolutely marvellous… great… doing all the things I never had time to do. The second year "scrap heap syndrome" set in, and I thought, "Oh, my God, I'm going mad." I have come to the conclusion, the Victorians had something - if you've never been out to work, you don't miss it. In other words, if you just graduate from being sweet little girl to being sweet little woman…

So I was going crackers, and I was still active, but I didn't want to do any of this do gooderish work, you know. I didn't particularly like conventional "charity work." Then one day a friend of mine said, "Why don't you try the hospice?" I didn't see how I could help there. However, much to my delight, I was proven wrong. I gave readings. I sat at the desk. I sent begging letters to various places – thank you's – and that sort of thing. But it really was a lifesaver as far as I was concerned. It made me feel less useless. When I think of old age, uselessness must be the worst. The boys were both reared - nobody needed me.

And I think this is a lovely story myself, but when I was seeing him [Gerard, her eldest son] off, I was up at Aldergrove, and he went off somewhere, you see. And this lovely girl came over to me, and she was wearing a red trouser suit – lovely looking girl, beautiful colour – very dark. And she said, "Hello, Mrs. McArdle, you don't know me," or "You don't remember me," and I said, "I'm sorry, I don't." "I was your pupil, and you taught me at St. Brigid's." And I said, "What are you doing up here?" "Well," she said, "the folks have all emigrated to Toronto." And she said, "I was just back, tidying up a few things in town." So I introduced them, and that was that. She was the best thing that ever happened to Gerard. And they have a fine son, another John, now in his teens.

John [her youngest son] grew up in a very difficult time. They had it very tough. You were terrified if they went out - you were terrified if they stayed in, 'cause I remember one night John said to me he was going to a party. And I said, " Oh John." "Oh, it's all right; it's all right. It's a very respectable party, Mama. It's great." And I said, "John darling, it's not *that* I'm worried about." Well we never knew when someone would be blown up or shot or caught in an ambush, so his generation, I think, had it tough. When Gerard was growing up, one worried about too many parties and things like that. But by the time John was in his teens, one worried about bombs and shootings and constant danger.

In fact, John had to sit his finals against the background of the UWC Strike, which paralysed the whole province – no heat, no light, no transport, no shops, no hotels. It wasn't lovely for poor old John, because how did he get to Queens to sit his finals, literally across town? One of his friends, Brian Delany, set out at dawn and went round the mountain. But at that time there was a hotel - I think that it's long gone - called the Russell Court. And I rang them, and they were a bit chary – "We aren't really taking guests." And I said, "Well, I know you're not, but this is just for one night." So they said, "Yes." That was the first night of his exams, so he stayed over there that night – so no problem then. The second day of the exams, I rang again. "Sorry, we've been instructed to close." So I went into my domineering act! It managed to go all right, you know. And he went over that night – no light, no heat, no food. But at least he was on the doorstep for his finals.

We [teachers] couldn't get to school. So the Ministry in its wisdom ordained that you were to go to the nearest school – sort of count your time – with the result that I ended up in Holy Family which was just 'round the corner from Atlantic Avenue – a primary school. I thought I wouldn't like primary teaching. And I was right. I suppose they never thought of telling the wee fellas that [they wouldn't have their regular teacher]. I have never felt such waves of animosity from those scraps. And it only dawned on me – they thought I was going to replace their own beloved teacher whom they adored, naturally enough. You know what primary kids are like. You could feel the weight of dislike, and it suddenly dawned on me, you see, and I said, "Oh, I wonder, could it be that, 'cause I hadn't done anything?" And I said, "By the way," I said, " I want you to help me now and tell me how Miss… I've forgotten her name… Brown does things, because remember, I'm only here to help her, and I don't really know very much." Oh, after that, they took me to their hearts – fine so long as I wasn't going to do them out of their teacher. The other funny part is that most Catholic schools, including my own, were staffed by Protestants and vice versa, because we were the nearest. Isn't that lovely?

[Early in the Troubles, John was taken to a house at the top of Atlantic Avenue to be questioned.] In spots, it's vivid, but by and large it's blurred. I remember there had been trouble brewing. [This was during the time of Internment.] We were more or less waiting for it, and I remember that night, I had gone to bed. John had gone to bed, and Gerard, of course, was away, thank God. He was already in Canada. And I heard knocking and banging, which was not unusual, and I wakened John. And shortly after that, of course, clattering at the door and they were into all the houses. And there were several soldiers, and they sort of charged around the place. They took all the men between, I suppose, about 15 and 50, up to a house at the corner of Atlantic Avenue for interrogation, and this fellow, whose name I think was Kent, stayed with me. And apparently they left a soldier, I suppose, in each house. But you didn't know whether the boys were coming back or not. But thank God, he did, and I made no further comment about it… most ridiculous thing… I said, "Right, we'll go to bed now."

But the next day was a little bit bemused in school, because I really was still stunned by the whole thing. But I noticed from then on, that it was a peculiar thing, we never had such good discipline in the school, because the kids, quite a few from New Lodge, were scared out of their wits. School was a haven, you know. They were safe in school. Nobody was going to come near them. So that was really all that happened, and that would have been early on in the Troubles. It was not nice at all – well, I'm not saying anything everybody doesn't know, but oh, the anxiety – it was awful. It really was. And most of the boys took flight, got out - Catholic boys, I'm talking about now – innocent ones. I'm sure there were a lot who weren't.

It [the disruption of ordinary life] became so much the order of the day that you really were not aware of it. At the height of it when there was bombing every day, businesses going up all over the place and getting out of town just in time – which was standard practice - a friend of mine, Roisin Kennedy's sister, came in. She was a solicitor in town. She came in from work. And her mother had the television on, and as Mary took off her coat, she asked, "Anything new?" And her mother, still looking at the news, said, "Yeah, there was a man shot on the Shankill." And Mary heard herself saying, "Just one?" And then she said, "Oh, my God, what am I saying?" But that was the reaction. And everybody I knew just wanted all your young people out… but particularly if they were boys, because they were definitely not safe. I mean the young couples were bombed coming home from Queens. They were beaten up. So what's new?

There was one old lady – I'm an old lady now – lived near me, and she said one day (there was somebody who had been bombing or half a dozen were killed or something like that), and she said, "Ach, love, they were fightin' when I was born, and they'll be fightin' when I die." And she was right. I don't think it'll ever stop. And of course at the head of Atlantic Avenue there was always rioting. That was when I knew I lived in north Belfast.

Now that was a stinker – the UWC Strike. That was terrifying - absolutely terrifying – quite apart from the fact that it was extremely uncomfortable, because we had no food. We'd no bread. We'd no milk. And I'll never forget… just shows how divorced nuns are from anything going on… but at the height of it, you know, when you didn't know whether your house would be there when you went home or not, the principal called a staff meeting. Can you imagine? And there we were sitting… didn't give a damn if the school went up in smoke. So as I say, that was particularly frightening and men in lorries and businesses closed. I even forget how long it lasted, but it was bad. It's never mentioned now, though I suppose it was a bit of a watershed. You deliberately forget it. It would be just a repetition, because it went on for so long.

One thing I do remember… I think I told you about Maureen McKinney. She has a son – Joe is the same age as John, and they were very close friends. Joe became a priest and was in training in Rome. And he came home from Rome, and Maureen threw her arms around him and said, "Oh, Joe love, it's so lovely to see you. When are you going back?" In other words we loved to see them, but we wanted to get them away again.

Well… nothing will ever change, I don't think. I think it's too ingrained. Well, I can't see where the hope would come from, because the Catholic community has been forced to dig in again. I mean, we've become as embattled as we ever were. The Protestant community are still convinced that England wants them, and I don't think she does. And the south doesn't want either of us. Would you, if you were a southerner doing well and on the pig's back or on the back of the tiger? I don't know where that phrase came from, by the way. But would you want the north? I wouldn't - we'd only be a liability. So, you know, where's the solution going to come from? I don't believe in that [hope] anymore. You can't help becoming rather cynical. So often over the 30 years, you know, things have happened - not with me it doesn't happen anymore - but things used to happen, and you'd say, "Oh great, you know, maybe this is a breakthrough - maybe this is it." Then bingo. And just today the same thing has happened again. It looked as if things were moving. We were behaving in a civilized fashion. Nobody is actually getting killed, but people are ignoring the fact, for instance, that churches are being ransacked all over the place, that homes are being targeted and shots fired into them, that people are being beaten up. Simply because bombs aren't going off, people think there's peace here. That's - to put it mildly - that's short sighted, because it's not. I mean, guns are coming from somewhere.

The Irish are nostalgic for what they can't have and grieve that their lives are not what they thought they would be. We seem unable to live in the present. [Lillian found a poem in her notebook which illustrates this point well.]

We look before and after,
And pine for what is not.
Our sincerest laughter

With some pain is fraught.
Our sweetest songs are those
That tell of saddest thought.

[Her son John showed an early interest in civil rights.] I think it was just the atmosphere, you know... it could have been a mixture of things. Well, he was a Catholic. He was a North of Ireland Catholic. He was a reasonably well-educated north of Ireland Catholic. His mother was non-political! Maybe I wasn't as non-political as I thought, but officially I'm non-political. As I said before, I'm not a republican in the Irish sense. I know to a stranger that must sound awfully funny. And he also had a great-uncle who was a civil rights lawyer. My uncle, Colm McAteer... I didn't realize that probably that had quite an effect on John, because he was in the post office when there weren't a lot of Catholics in the post office, and he did law sort of on the side. And then he did pro bono work from that on. It wasn't called civil rights then. But things like, you know - Catholic emancipation and that sort of thing. And I think probably John inherited an interest from it there. Certainly he's been devoted to it ever since. And then of course his own life – he was at Queens at the height of it. You don't forget things like that. And, as I say, most mothers of my generation just wanted our boys to get the best education they could, and get them out – which is why Northern Ireland is so denuded. But people are coming back now - why I don't know. I mean my elder boy, Gerard, would come back at the drop of a hat, and I would like him to, because he sees Belfast as he knew it, and it wasn't as troubled. You see there are six and a half years between them. So Gerard knew a quite different Belfast than John did. Gerard had what would be a normal teenage – too many dances and that sort of thing. Poor old John couldn't go to a dance.

It was funny when they were here, John's son, Peter – he was over with me one day, you see - and he said, "Nana, can I ask you something?" And I said, "Sure you can, Peter." He's very solemn. He's John all over the world. He said, ""Oh I was just wondering does it annoy you that you can't hear very well anymore?" I thought, "God love the wee soul. He really is sympathetic." And I said, "Well, you know it does, Peter. It annoys me quite a lot. Why do you ask?" "Well, I just thought I'd ask, because it annoys me having to say things twice!" But he really is a pet, you know. So they were here for a year, and that was very nice. Young Lisa [granddaughter] rang the other day. I lifted the phone, and I got, "Lisa heah. I just wanted to thank you, Nana." She had a birthday recently, you see. "Well, actually, Nana, the skirt was a little bit wide, but Mama can take it in."

[As one gets older] you begin to wonder a trifle about the hereafter. My friends are really all very rude. One of them said to me, "Well, at least you'll be warm," because I'm always cold here. So I can't think what she meant, of course! I don't know what part faith has played in her life. I think probably a lot, but it must have been sub-conscious or almost, because I'm not what my mother used to call an "altar crawler." The older I grow, the less patience I have with organized religion – to a great extent, my own. I sometimes think that the Catholic Church - at least the Catholic Church here as an institution - seems to me to bear singularly little resemblance to the One who founded it. I think I could claim – I would like to think I could claim – to being a Christian in that I admire Christ. But whether I'm still a confirmed Catholic, I don't know, and I don't know where we suddenly became "Catholic." Oh a favourite quote of mine (I think it's Ogden Nash) - "Organized charity, carefully iced, in the name of a cautious, statistical Christ." Isn't that lovely? And unfortunately, it's very true. So, as I say, I don't know - I honestly don't know. I often wonder, would I be more honest to ask, "I'm not a Catholic?" but then nobody gives a damn whether I am or not.

But as I say, I honestly don't know. I once said flippantly [about the afterlife] that at least I'd be warm, and a friend added, "And think of the nice people you'll meet!" So as I say, my spirituality or my religion or whatever it 'tis, I don't know - I honestly don't know. I think probably it may have played a greater role in my life than I'm aware of. But I've disagreed - well, I'm too old now to bother disagreeing - heartily with very many Catholics. I can't think I've ever disagreed heartily with a Protestant. But of course then that needs clarification too, because oddly enough as I said to John one day, I said, "John, you know, I now have more Protestant friends than I have Catholic friends – or certainly as many." And he said, "That's great," and I said, "But you don't realise how great." Again I don't want to blame our religion for it, but that's one reason why I would be for integrated education. Because even at Queens, I was still very much the convent girl, you know.

In fact, it wasn't even Queens. It was when I was working in the censorship, and all our supervisors were English, naturally enough, and there was one – a Mrs. Brook-Rose. I met her one day, and I stood back, as one would, and she said, "Oh, thanks so much, Miss O'Neill. I always say one can tell a convent-bred gal." And I was not quick enough or sophisticated enough to point out that it wasn't the convent gave me my good manners. It was my own family. But, as I say, even then I didn't have any close Protestant friends. I have now, thank God. Because we didn't mix - even in Queens we didn't mix a lot, which I think was a shame. I met some of them in the censorship. I met quite a few of them through the hospice – volunteer in the hospice – which I can't do very much now, and just seem to have run into them. You know, I never remember sort of actually saying, "I am meeting a Protestant..." sort of thing.

If anything, I suppose I'm an old age feminist. And, I mean, women were certainly not properly treated in the Catholic Church or anywhere else for that matter. Women are much better educated now and are showing more independence in every field, including the church. But I think it's not that they're showing more independence. I think the church doesn't realise - it's just that they're ignoring it, which is a lot more dangerous. Because if you ignore a thing, it's dead, but it doesn't know it's dead. Isn't that true?

You know, intermarriage was frowned on - again, rather like the States, when you see marriage between coloureds and whites. Here Protestant and Catholic didn't marry a lot...well they did, but they weren't suppose to. It's only comparatively recently that Catholics were permitted to attend Protestant funerals, a Protestant wedding. And that's ridiculous, because what I can't understand is, if your belief is so frail that it means somebody else is going to adulterate it, it's not worth having in the first place. That's my father and mother, of course. So as I say, I think it's much better in some ways now, but then I feel so sorry for people who have intermarried, and now they're suffering for it politically...not from their respective churches. I mean, I always think of those three children who died in Ballymoney as a result of Drumcree. What did that advance anybody anywhere?

[Lillian's cross-community interest is expressed well in this poem she found in an old notebook.]

Song For the Twelfth of July
Come pledge again thy heart and hand,
One grasp that ne're shall sever;
Our watch word be – "Our native land!"
Our motto – "Love forever."
And let the orange lily be
Thy badge, my patriot brother.
The everlasting green for me;
And we for one another.
THOMAS DAVIS

Pauline

Pauline has spent her entire life living in the Clonard area of Belfast. She remembers the blitzes of World War II as well as the burning of Bombay Street. Raising one child alone, she provided for her family by working in a mill. She is now 71 years old and lives in a fold.

My first recollection as a child was the morning my sister was born and there was nearly four years between her and I. I remember a full tin of biscuits, and every time I see a tin of biscuits as an adult, it reminds me that is the first thing I can remember. My mammy always would have everything in for the baby. She always had a cake and her bottle of whiskey, and her bottle of wine, and a tin of biscuits, and lemonade for children. When she tried to pay the nurse, the nurse said, "Look, goodness sake, Bella, wait until your baby's born before you pay."

I had four sisters. I was the fourth of five children, and my father had a hairdresser's shop - a barber's shop - and we lived at the back of the barber's shop. My granny would have come up to mind us. My mummy would maybe have went out to work sometimes. She was a weaver at the local factory. My father… he had a good wee business… but his heart wasn't good. Sometimes Mummy would have given him medication at night, and that was to kill pain. But he survived till he was 57. But we were the children of his second marriage. Mummy and Daddy were both married twice. Mummy was married when she was 19, and she was a widow before she was 20, because her husband went to the navy - First World War. The war was only on six weeks, and his boat was torpedoed. She had no family now. My daddy had two children, and one of them was a cot death, and one of the other had meningitis… and then his wife died. My daddy never had a son - seven children, but he never had a son.

I didn't like school. I had to be trailed down into school, I was that stubborn. I was a very young child, about four or five. I went to St. Vincent's School, down Clonard Street, and then there was a wee shop called Russell's. They made their own candy - homemade candy - and they had candy apples and sweets. Then there was a wee shop called Kitty Green's at the corner, and Kitty had a wee bell at her door and a wee latch and she sold wee story books and all - and jotters and pencils and sweets and sticks for a fire and everything. I wasn't the brightest at school, because I am partially hearing now, and I think my hearing was bad then too. I had two perforated eardrums. But I was always good at talking and not minding me own business - seeing what everybody else was doing!

I went to school 'til I was 14 - ten years. Oh aye, you couldn't have left then until you were 14. I never got any certificates anyway unless you went to the grammar school. There was nothing to prove that you were there. Then I started work in the Albion - the war was on then - then the war was over, and the work went down. Rather than look for another job, I just stayed back to the pressing. That's how I became a presser in the Albion. I was in the Albion for 48 years. I suppose you could have went to other jobs, but it was constant.

Then I got married, and then my husband left me. I had one child, and I had to go out to work. I was married in 1952, and she wasn't born until 1955, so like it wasn't a rush thing. My husband... you called him John... and he was a good worker. He worked like in a butcher factory. He had a good job. But then we had no home. We were living with my mother and my sister. I think that life wasn't very pleasant for him. It would have been pleasant enough for me, because it was my own home, but then whenever I was looking for a home, he wasn't interested. He met this other girl, and he went away with her. That was 1958. That is 42 years.

He is in Coventry, and last year my daughter went over to see him, and I don't know how she looked him up. They recognised one another and got on well together. So she didn't go to his house - she just went in the café, and she says to him about his partner. He never told her he wasn't married, and she says, "Well, why did you not marry after divorcing my mother? Why did you not marry your partner?" He says he couldn't marry anybody outside the Catholic Church. Now wasn't he awful good? He would love to see me, but I wouldn't be fussed.

As far as I am concerned, I am not divorced... as far as I feel... and so I contested the divorce. It cost me money. I got £3 by the way - a pound for her and £2 for me - that was it - that was the magistrate's thing. I had to go to a downtown office to pick up the money - every Saturday. And some Saturdays you went down, and the money wasn't there. I was getting no money for groceries, because I was working. My mother wouldn't have let you sit in the house. My mother said no way would she wait on any man supporting her. If she had her trade, she would be out using it.

Me and my sister [lived with Pauline's mother], and she died of a brain haemorrhage at 41. Mummy died in 1971. I lost two good friends - lost one in 1967 and one in 1971. I have three more sisters, and we are very supportive to one another.

[One of Pauline's co-workers could not pay her electric bill.] Years ago they would have cut your electric off, if you hadn't it paid. And I said, "Tell you what I will do," I says, "I will go home in the dinner hour and get the money off my mammy." It was my own money I was giving, but you had to say that to get her to pay you back. And I says, "My mammy will lend me for you." So, I paid her electric bill, but she didn't appreciate it. I pitied them, because they [Protestant co-workers] couldn't communicate with us. They wouldn't befriend you, for they were afraid of somebody knowing. I always reached out to them. She gave me it [the borrowed money] back again. I took my stand with them like. I mean to say, I stood up to them. I wouldn't let them belittle me, no. What I used to say was, "You couldn't wipe my boots." I had my pride, ah yes, I had. But I cared for them. I cared for them, you know. I saw them as people. I didn't see them as a Protestant or a Catholic. I just saw them as people. I would have done them a good turn, because my father used to say, "If you can't do a good turn, walk away from it. If you can't say a good word, don't say anything."

Rita [Pauline's daughter] went to St. John's school and done very well. But every time I used to see this teacher that taught her, she used to say to me, "Rita would do well at St. Rose's." She qualified herself. Her work brought her in. She was there until she was 18. She took her A Levels out of St. Rose's. She was very popular.

And then she went on to the college - then she graduated at Queen's [in teacher training]. She didn't get into the teaching, because that year there was an awful lot of cutbacks. By the way, she got two degrees. That was the Master's and Bachelor's – in counselling and guidance. Then she went into youth work. And she saw this advert - anybody taught marginal children. The children up around West Belfast would be marginal. And so she got the job as a school inspector - anything that is funded from the Belfast Council Library Board.

Well I am proud of Rita. I am indeed. But she is saying, no the pride goes to her for me. She was down inspecting the schools somewhere in the province, and she saw a friend, and God, they were kissing one another. Then the head teacher found out she was an inspector. "Well," she says, "that is the first time I have ever saw a teacher kissing an inspector!" I have two grandchildren. I have one called Niamh and one called Kieran.

I am not a true republican like, you know. I think their ideals was all right, but the way they went about it... When the trouble was on the Shankill... I don't want people on the Shankill to be suffering. I would feel for the other side, I really would. But I know they wouldn't be as wicked - republicans to each other. Now I have spoke out, and I have give off stick. But they let you have your opinion more.

I remember Bombay Street. I remember being on the Shankill Road on the 12th of August, and I was going up there for her [Rita's] uniform. Sylvia's was on the Shankill Road and on the corner of North Howard Street. It runs off the Shankill Road onto the Falls. And I said to Mummy, "Oh I will not be back on the Shankill again." It was so bleak, and there was nobody on it. It was just like a war was coming. Hell was let loose in Derry. That was 1959 - the Apprentice Boys marched in Derry, but the Bogside was waiting on them. The police - I suppose they turned their backs on whatever they were doing. You see, it is the RUC is our trouble. If the RUC changed, you would see the armed guards changing. You would see the ordinary Protestant changing then. They are the culprits.

My mummy, my sister and her friend used to come down to see us every Thursday night, and they came down that Thursday, and they left early. We were getting all the blast on the Falls, and everybody was running about. There was no army in then, and there was no police, for they locked themselves in the barracks and never came out. And all that night, I was making tea.

We always had a bonfire on the 15th of August, and they carried wood and all. Rita would have had a guitar, and she was going to play the guitar round the bonfire. They made a barricade of the bonfire wood at the bottom of the street. Father Houston and Harry Connolly came round, and they said take it down, because the Mackies were going to work the next morning. We took the barricade down. There wasn't a gun. There was only stones what they were throwing, and mine was throwing it back at them.

And then they were hammering the windows up. And Mummy says to me, "Now, tonight you and I will stay here, but we will send her [Rita] down to Josie." That is my sister and her husband. "We will send her down to the Springfield Avenue, so she will be out of the road." That morning my cousin came up. He was in Ardoyne all night. And he says, "Ach you will have to go out." And she [Mummy] says, "But I didn't get out in the 20s." But he says, "This isn't the 20s, believe you me."

But they [the security forces] got orders to shoot into Divis Flats, and they were ordered to shoot everywhere else. There is an old woman - Aunt Min - was in the tower, and one of the tower flats is all bullets where they were shooting all round Aunty Min. Well Aunty Min couldn't hear, and they knew there was an old woman in that flat, and they shot into that flat all night. That's why they can't do decommissioning. They couldn't decommission. They couldn't let them sit without a gun. They can't leave us to the mercy of the RUC, because we have had enough. The Orange Lodge is behind them. They are all in the Orange Lodge.

Then that night hell let loose. Tilly Culbert went to pay her rent for a month, and when Tilly came back she had no house. She hadn't a stick of furniture - everything was up in a big bonfire. The chapel bell rung at four o'clock for the people to get out. By this time I was away, because I was away at my sister's, and we [my mammy and Rita and my other sister] were the first out. We were away for a week. So I really didn't see anything that night.

And the army came in. I never saw the army coming in. The army came in at six o'clock, and they made camp. But I didn't see the army till the next day when I came down again. But, it was terrible - a big bonfire. We weren't even expecting that.

[Pauline remembers Internment during WWII] - in Crumlin Road, and there was also a ship... I think they called it the Arata ship, and there were all young men on it, and most of them fell into TB, because there was no nutrition on it, and the rats was running everywhere. And there was people had to go down. They spent money to go down to see them and probably take them food and maybe bring them a change of clothing or something. And the same in the Crumlin Road. They had to go up - take them stuff up there.

They would have been enemies of the crown, you see. Matter of fact, I had a cousin, and he worked in Telephone House. Telephone House was like BT now. You see they tried to bring out conscription here. But people from Northern Ireland - ones who wanted to go to fight - could be conscripted to fight for Britain. So anyway, he would have been one of the ones that would have been conscripted, for he worked for the Imperial Government. He refused, so he got 24 hours to get out. Internees were kept in prison until after the war, unless they signed a paper. Oh, he didn't sign anything. If they didn't do anything, they were just suspects. So he went away to his house, and I think he joined the southern Army, and then that marriage was split up. His wife wouldn't go down, and he couldn't come up here, so that was that.

[Pauline remembers the blitzes of World War II.] I must have been about 12. And, well there was a Monday night blitz and being so near Mackies and industrial parts - of course they knew where that was. And Mackies was set on fire about a hundred times that night. Were we up? No, we were sleeping. We slept through it. We slept through raids and all with soldiers. We slept through the air raid and everybody made a laugh of it, because we were always ready to go when the all clear sounded. We didn't sleep through the big Tuesday night blitz. There was a landmine come through here, and it landed at Cupar Street. And there were a lot of people killed and all. So after that we had the vaults. If you go down steps beyond those railings there [points], that is the vault where police were buried. It is an underground thing. So Father McNiffe went down to Cupar Street and brought all up - told the Protestants that if they wanted refuge or anything just to come up there, and they did.

Kathleen Hunter [was killed in the blitz]. She was a chum of a woman that lived beside us, and she wanted her to stay that night. She says, "No," she would go home. And she went home, and they were all killed, except one - the whole family. That was over the Antrim Road. They got it too - they were coming up over the coast, you know.

During the Troubles, it was burning buses, and you had to walk to work. This went on and on. A friend of mine, Kathleen Donnelly - she had a limp - and she had to run away during the bomb warning. Then at night the buses were off, and she had to walk it home. Her mummy was anxious for her coming home, wondering what was going to happen. And you never knew... when you came to the bus stops, there was no buses. There was nobody there to tell you that there was no buses, and then there was no black taxis. They didn't go up the Grosvenor Road - they all went up the Falls. And there was one night I was carrying these sticks home to light the fire, and then I thought, "No buses." Well I could have carried those sticks on the black taxi. As a matter of fact, I was going to phone a black taxi. I was so angry. I am sure my language was choice. I got so angry and so frustrated. I was tired after working, and the black taxis flying up and down and no buses. I wouldn't take a black taxi like. No way would I support them.

I know a whole lot of workers that lived round here, and we had to up and walk home again. Sometimes you couldn't have walked up the Grosvenor Road. You had to make another detour, away round the town and up the Falls, because there was something on the Grosvenor Road. [To travel that distance] now it is about half an hour - then it would be two hours. I couldn't do it now. And that was one thing I didn't like - the transport.

I remember one night we were on the bus, and the Protestants were on our buses too. I am sure they were nervous going up round the Grosvenor Road to Springfield. And I see him yet. They were hijacking the bus - everybody was tired and weary. This girl I knew lived on the West Circular, and I left her half way home in case something would happen to her, walking up the Springfield. I was worried for her. They just burned the buses. I remember one year, I must

Burned out homes on Bombay Street.

have walked it for nine weeks, and rain running out of me. That was with good shoes and all on, but you had to take them off and dry them. Like I was in my what – 50s. Thirty years that went on and off.

I'll tell you about the 13 dead in Derry. That was Bloody Sunday. And I went to work that Monday. They were all chat, chat chitting and all - oh God, calling the IRA this and calling the IRA that - but there was no word about the people they shot, like. And that night I came out of work, and there wasn't a light from the Sandy Row. The only lights you would have saw was the lights for the hospital. And there was shots fired. I think they shot a soldier or something at that stage. And one person stopped me and asked me for a cigarette, and I says, "You can take them, because I will be able to get them when a couple of bars are open," as the bars never closed. I was really afraid. You didn't know what was going to break out. I never met another person from Leeson Street 'til I got home. See whenever I got home, I could have kissed the ground. I was so glad to be safe in my own home.

My house was raided once, and I was up at my daughter's house. I was minding the children then. "Oh," she said, "the soldiers are here." I said, "What is the soldiers doing at my house?" She said, "They are in all the houses." They had the very grate out and the door was broke. And then there was a gun found, not in my house, two doors down. The young fella, he was charged, but he got off like, and you want to see that house. The water was running out of bust pipes and everything. In the earlier days now, they [security forces] would have come, and they stole things from people - like lifted maybe a watch or something, but then the time came when you had to search them before they went out. You were allowed to do that.

[Speaking of the UWC Strike] Oh, God bless us. That came in March 1974. But that UWC strike we were off - it was wintertime. And the electric was off, and we all cooked our food in the yard - a wee grill and two bricks and coal and made our stew or whatever we were getting. Like it was great, and I had a fire upstairs in my bedroom. We could have lit it and made something there, but then the big one - the big strike - it fell in June. It lasted about six weeks, I think.

That first strike - I wasn't working that morning, and I went to get my hair done or something. I went down to the Albion there, and they were all out on strike. And all I got was my maintenance money. That was all I was getting, because she [Rita] was still at college. In 1974 she was still at school. Yes, she had left St. Rose's, and she was at Queen's. In between Queen's and the college, and that was all I had. But we got on all right. And then our gas was off...

well, the Shankill was off. And you see when the electric went off and our lights went out, their lights was out. They got away with that - they really got away with it.

The purpose of the strike was to bring down the government. The loyalist strike was to bring that down. You see the shipyard and the power station and all essentials – they [Protestants] were in the majority. All they had to do was bring them all out on strike, and Ulster was never the same from it, because that was when all the investment and all was taken out.

I wouldn't have had much experience of being harassed, like - I wouldn't. And even in the street like, I wasn't stopped much to see where you were going. Oh, some people were. Well, I am going back to 1948 or 1949. My husband and I were standing talking in Cupar Street. A policeman came along and he says to me, "What is your name?" And I said, "What reason have you to ask me my name?" I says, "I'll not tell you until you tell me what I have done or supposed to have done." And I wouldn't tell him my name or address. My husband told, but I didn't.

You didn't want your name on their files at all because I had a niece, and the army brought her away in the early hours - six o'clock one morning - and they brought her to a holding station. They told her about her aunts - her two aunts were in the Cumann na mBán. That was the women part of the IRA. They told her about her uncle. He was buried in Glasnevin, and he was out with the Citizen Army - he was with McSweeney - told her all that and told her how many shots and all was fired over his coffin. Now she didn't know that - her father didn't know that, because her aunts were way dead before he even would have grew up - because they had a file in the barracks. And they had all that on her. But she says, "I don't know my aunt." Oh they were all apologies like. It was the wrong person. You see her name wasn't in the barracks at all, but her aunt's was.

It will be a long time [until there is peace]. Yes, there will be, because there is no other way out. Like nobody wants to go back, and the people on the Shankill... but I mean it is quiet now on the Shankill. I was talking to a woman this morning from the Shankill, and she says it's quiet. You see they started that I think to get the Provos out, so that they could say they have broke the Agreement. They said that the IRA broke their windows and all, and they done that themselves.

James

Jim Snoddy is a life-long Quaker. He and his wife, Betty, owned their own business and parented three sons. He reflects on being a pacifist during a civil war. Jim is in his 70s and lives in east Belfast.

I was born in Belfast in a house on the Ormeau Road, just above the bridge. It was a semi-detached. All the other houses, apart from our block, were terraced houses. My mother and father were married in 1922. I was born in 1927. We had no real difficulty with food or clothing, but every penny had to be watched. From 1922 to 1938 my father wasn't in regular employment that brought in a steady income. In 1938 he was re-employed as a clerk in Harland and Wolff. I think I heard that the house had actually been given to them. We had rich relations who were in the linen business – the Sintons. My mother was a Sinton.

It took me a long time to really appreciate my mother and father. I wish I would have given more time to them when it was possible to do that. I have a few lines about my father. At age 42 the words of poems began coming to me. I could not write anything until that age.

Deep in my father
Was a loving kindness,
A caring for the unfortunate,
A despising of ostentation.
Deep in me, be as my father
That I might honour his name.

And another one about my father:
I know my father
Through all of me.
My scrappy scribble
His copper plate.
My good health
Compared to breathless asthma.
I have known affluence.
His time was the 30s,
Struggling, disappointing years.

Jim and Betty on their tandem bicycle (circa late 40s).

Through all of me
A loving deepness grows,
Making us as one.

And one about my mother – I saw a child being lifted up and realised I had
been lifted in the same way:
I think I remember
A time before remembering.
The loveliness in the lifting
When learning to walk.
A hug and perhaps a kiss.
My mother's hopes and fears
Centered in me.
All this was mine
Through difficult, penny-pinching years.

The next one is called "Post Office Savings Book:"
I remember with affection
A post office savings book
Given to me by my mother
Just before I was married –
A book unknown to me
Inscribed with my name and in credit.
A book, almost miraculously preserved
Through difficult and penny-pinching years.
A book lovingly added to in anticipation
Of my adulthood.
This I remember with affection
And with deep gratitude.

I went to the nearest primary school, called "elementary" at that time, which
was maybe a quarter of a mile away. I was certainly less than happy at this
school. They had a system where the headmaster did a tour each morning with
a cane in his hand, and we got 20 spellings. If you had any more than two
wrong, you got one slap - four you got two slaps on the hand. And we also had
tables, and we had a slapping rate for the tables as well. It didn't really
encourage people like me, although everything was meant with the best will in
the world. I have no reason to think that teachers were doing anything other

than what they considered to be the very best thing they could for you.

There had been enough money left in Quaker bursary funds for Friends' School, Lisburn, which meant a secondary grammar school education. If you were a Quaker at that time, you neither needed brains or money to go to Friends' School. I remember my mother talking about me going and being very excited. So I went to Friends' School when I was 11 years old and was there as a boarder from 1938 until 1945. I was very excited about going, and I didn't find school easy, but when I look back on it, there were really dedicated teachers. There were very good teachers in the sense that they never gave up on anybody. They never lost hope no matter how hopeless you were!

In school we played hockey and rugby and cricket. I was on the rugby team but not on either the cricket or the hockey team. I won the middle boys' championship at school. That's in athletics - I'm not certain whether it was a bad year for the competitors, but I won it! I was privileged that I was able to go to Friends' School. When I get a bit uptight about being on too many Quaker committees, I try to tell myself, "Remember Friends' School and the people who sat on Quaker committees to keep it going."

Kenneth Clay, who taught French, took us youth hostelling. It was a very important thing to me. I remember going away on a trip with him about 30 miles out to the Mourne Mountains – Slievenaman Youth Hostel. I met Kenneth many years later, and he asked me did I still remember it? And I said, "I remember it like yesterday." We had a few youth hostelling trips, and these were marvellous times. My sense of adventure was fulfilled and gave me something I could continue. When Betty and I met first, we had a tandem bike and still have it. We went youth hostelling when saving up to get married, so it was quite an influence on my life. It all came about through Friends' School.

I had one brother and one sister – an older brother and a younger sister. My brother started work in the "Newsletter" at 12 shillings a week which is 60p present money, but if you do the inflation rate on it, it's still only 30 pounds a week today. So that's what he had. We didn't talk a lot in our family one to another, but there was love in it.

I remember my mother telling me I was going to get a new sister before my sister was born. She couldn't have known whether it was a boy or girl. I remember thinking I was getting a full-sized girl, the same size as the girls that were running about the street.

We lived in a street that was all Protestant except one family opposite - the Duffy Family. He was a sergeant in the police. There was very little said in our house which could have been taken as being anti-Catholic. But there was some talk, I think, about the convent up the road – what went on behind the walls. It wasn't a dominant thing. And I remember at one time, meeting some boys and playing with them on what was known as the brick fields. And they were telling about the horrors of the Catholic Church, and all I knew is, I wasn't the same as the rest, and I wondered if I was a member. I remember my father bringing little homemade fretwork toys to the Catholic children's home up the road. This was not talked about very much, but certainly it was done with the very best of goodwill and received as such.

I went to Quaker Meeting from presumably about five. The Sunday school I think was between 10 and 20 pupils. The main thing I remember was the Christmas party which was a pretty big event in our lives - walking into a brightly decorated room with a large Christmas tree. And although we had sufficient, to see tables with as many cakes on it as you liked to eat was a little bit different from home. The Sunday school party was actually run by an organisation called the Band of Hope. The Band of Hope was a total abstinence organisation, and I have never taken alcohol.

I went to Frederick Street [Quaker Meeting] and have a slight memory of going down there and seeing an armoured car, probably in the 30s sometime. None of our family were particularly politically motivated. My mother had a very low opinion of anybody who was any way left wing. She liked my dad all right – or did at the start anyway! And my father was very much on the labour side of things. And he was in the Independent Labour Party which at one time was the pacifist Labour Party. We had no relations in the Orange Order nor anyone in the Masonic Order. I think in one country Meeting there may have been a few members of the Orange Order. I had no idea about discrimination... we're talking about my young days.

I left school in 1945, the same time as the end of the war. My father had a bit of influence with someone who worked in timber control. He got me a job as an apprentice in a timber yard. I was unhappy – tears in my eyes sometimes. I was thoughtless about my mother and father on very limited means. It never occurred to me my priority should have been to try and earn money to help them.

It ended up all right. I wouldn't have any regrets. I eventually, in later years, got my own business going and was very fortunate in the sense that I was able to make my living and enjoyed working on my own for small suppliers without their own salesmen. I would offer to act part time for them, and they would pay me commission. You bought bricks in Dungannon and sold them to a builder in Belfast without actually handling them and made a small profit on it.

I was very lucky I didn't get any big bankrupt builders, but there were continual sprints for many years to the bank to get the money in on time to meet my cheques. But it always worked out, and Betty was a bookkeeper as well. At times we thought we might lose the house, but I paid my bills promptly during all my 30 business years. It was a fulfilling way to earn your living. I can tell you a poem about business:

There goes McCormick
Builder of a grosser sort,
Famous for your shouts and boasts.
But had I forgotten
When money had me by the throat,
You asked, although you knew,
Would I take payment on account
Before it's due.
McCormick, McCormick
Forgive me for I judged you
From the outside
Which is very far from true.

I met Betty when I was 19 - we met on our bicycles. And we went youth hostelling together, and it was a gradual thing. I think we got it right in marrying one another, and I think she thinks the same. In those years people didn't get married until they saved up money, so that took a long time. Betty's not a Quaker and hasn't joined and doesn't intend to join, but she is active in Quaker Meeting. She was a Presbyterian, and we had great adventures, cycling on the tandem bike over in Scotland or down to Kerry. We met in 1947 and were married in 1952. You had to save for years to get married. We had to wait quite awhile. We had to wait in ways which people mostly don't wait now. And I think that is probably the best way for marriage. So we were married in the Presbyterian Church, and Betty worked on for quite a few years. She was a bookkeeper, which was good whenever I started working on my own.

The oldest son is Andrew. He's a trade unionist joint secretary of what is the Northern Ireland Printers' Union. He had no interest in Quakers – is a jolly good son to us now and keeps in touch. Andrew left at an early age – must have been about 17 or 18 - and got a job as an apprentice printer. The middle boy, Mark, he went to university and got a degree in chemical engineering and works for Her Majesty's Pollution Authority. He lives in England. The youngest one, Timothy, works for a firm of wholesale stationers – loads lorries at night –

doesn't mind night work at all – was married in June 1999. We have four grandchildren - one adopted grandchild.

[During the bombing of Belfast in World War II] nobody connected with our family was injured. There were no bombs in fact in our end of town. I think there were three raids on Belfast. I was in Belfast for one of these and at Friends' School at Lisburn, eight miles from Belfast. I remember the black outs. You had to be very strict about that. But I was only 11 when the war started, and I can remember crying with joy when it was over, as a boy, because I thought, "There will be no more killing."

Well, I've never really been tested in that subject [pacificism]. I find that my attitude on it, I'm afraid, varies a bit according to the circumstances. When everybody begins getting very jingoistic, for some reason or other that seems to strengthen me in my pacifism. But, you know, you can get yourselves into various situations where you begin to wonder - is there any way out other than using force? So I haven't really been tested in that subject, but I'm quite certain, if I was faithful, that's the way I ought to be.

People have absolute beliefs on things like heaven and hell and the death of Jesus. I'd tell them I believe there is a Spirit, which we call God, which created this world. He maintains this world, and he sent His son, Jesus, into the world. And Jesus is very special and different from any other person, and He lived and He died, and He rose again. That's about as far as I can go other than I believe that if we, in the old terms, give our hearts to Jesus, He will come into our lives. And this, I think to some extent, has happened to me. And perhaps the things I don't know aren't that important. And also, above all things, Jesus taught that we should love our neighbours as ourselves, and to me that is the opposite of war. We will be given strength to do what is right. I would pray before many situations.

I see Quakerism as very much a Christian religion. I sometimes wish I was in a slightly more evangelical Meeting, but then our Meeting has changed and is more Christian based than what it used to be. I think Quakers are over democratic. And yet, I think there's a certain value in discussing things in open Meeting, but I do find a great deal of Quaker business trying. It has to be done, and it has to be done some way. But that is a part of Quakerism that I would tend to shy away from. But I don't just shy as far as I might! Somebody has to do it.

I was on the Peace Committee for many years, but I wasn't convener. But I remember one time we met with John Hume and some of the other people. John Hume requested a meeting with Quakers to see how an organisation could stop from slipping from a non-violent way to being taken over by violent people. He probably didn't get much of an answer. It helps to show you that he really wanted it non-violent rather than any other way. I'm on the Temperance Committee which is total abstainers' committee. I was brought up in that tradition - we were a non-drinking family. It was my mother and father's position on it. It was a tradition among Quakers at that time that alcohol was not taken. Although in our general Christian Council, to abstain is now largely ignored. Quakers are occasional drinkers. I could talk on about that subject - people who are much better Quakers than me and have an occasional drink. I've been clerk of the Frederick Street Meeting for many years. There is a business meeting once a month after Sunday Meeting. Any member can raise any matter they wish – no voting. The clerk judges the feeling of the meeting. It requires diplomacy. I've more or less been conscripted to Quaker committees. I feel nearer to God, not with being on Quaker committees but by playing a tune in an old people's home. [Jim plays a harmonica.]

I had arranged to be at an Alzheimer's centre outside Dublin. A wife visiting her husband with Alzheimer's decided to dance with him. And for a short time there was joy and laughter between them. I felt privileged that God had blessed me to give this small service.

Coming back on the train, there was a family - Mum and Dad and four youngsters - all pretty small. One youngster got a good telling off for running away and was bawling and crying away. So I said could I play the youngster a tune on the mouth organ, and it might stop? So I played the youngster a tune on the mouth organ, and the youngster was so amazed it shut up.

I need help to know what is conceit and what is service. There is a Quaker member who had MS all her life and had a stroke. We were brought up in Frederick Street together. I go and see her. She might be sleepy or she might want me to stay. I can do it better if I have a little prayer about it. God always gives me something to say. Those things are much more important to me than Quaker committees, although I'd better do the best I can with Quaker committees. I don't think I have anything I can give on committees, but there's a scarcity of people to go on committees - that's one of our problems.

I haven't lost anybody in the Troubles. I knew a foreman on a building site - he was shot. I knew the fella just through business. I knew of a neighbour of my brother's at Finaghy - they just walked into his office and shot him, because he was doing work for military. Well, I really haven't been affected at all. I've simply done my job, and at early days people like me perhaps and others thought there ought to be a Christian witness as to what we can do to get this stopped. You sort of puzzled it out, and you maybe joined the Alliance Party, or you went canvassing for the Alliance Party, and then you sort of began to think that about all you could do is to lead your life in compassion, kindness and love. So it really hasn't affected me very much at all. I haven't done very much either.

I remember little things like when Frederick Street was full of Catholic people, sitting up at night in the old Frederick Street Meeting House. I remember during Internment, people slept in South Belfast Meeting House. And I remember going into a Catholic area – Ballymurphy direction – helping to get children out and bringing them down to the Meeting House. I remember coming through City Cemetery, and I remember a little girl looking at a soldier or sailor's grave - "They get much better graves than we have." I felt so privileged to be of service in helping the children. So I've only been on the margins of anything like that.

I'm not at all sad about being 73. I'm grateful to my parents who cared for and loved me during difficult financial times – grateful to my Meeting at Frederick Street and their kindly persuasion to follow a religious life. I'm grateful to Friends' School – Lisburn – and their nurturing and finding value in all, including me. I'm grateful that I found acceptable work and was able to provide for Betty and the family. I feel gratitude for all these years of good health and am grateful that I found a lifetime companion in Betty, my wife. I am grateful for getting older.

What do I hope for? I hope to be able to do sing-a-longs for a few more years. I hope not to give trouble to anyone through illness or crankiness and to be able to care for Betty all her days. I want to live my remaining days in holy acceptance of all that life brings and to enter into the eternal presence of Jesus. And I would like to see love, peace and reconciliation in my home place of Northern Ireland.